Bill Mason's No Nonsense

Guide To Fly Fishing
In Idaho

Learn About Fly Fishing Idaho's
Finest Rivers, Streams, Lakes and Reservoirs

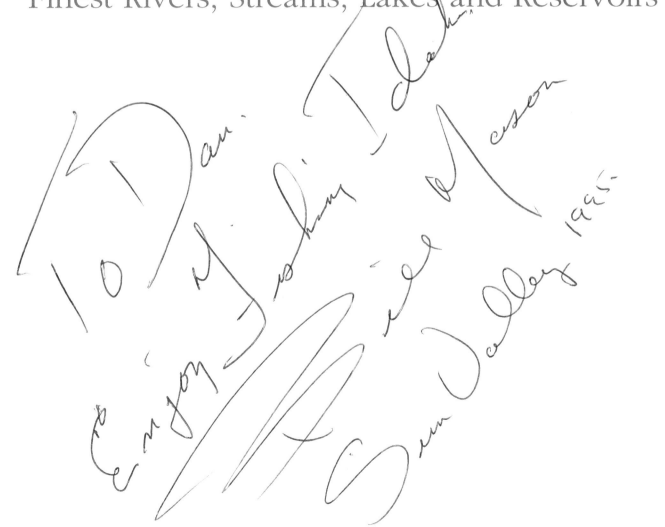

Acknowledgements

The author thanks the following people for their assistance and comments during this guide's production: My word processor friends Becky and Linda. Fly fishing experts Bill and Katie Howe and Jeff Perin. Author of the first "No Nonsense" guide Harry Teel and his word processing wife Dee. David Banks who came up with the idea and put things together. Lynn Perrault who made my maps tidy and designed the covers. Tom, Bridget and Patricia and the entire gang at Maverick Publications for formatting and printing. Steve Bly and Brad Teel for their photographs. The contributions of these people were of immeasurable value.

Bill Mason's No Nonsense Guide to Fly Fishing In Idaho
©1994 by David Communications
ISBN #0-9637256-1-0

Published and distributed by David Communications
6171 Tollgate • Sisters, Oregon • 97759 • U.S.A.

Printed by Maverick Publications, Inc.
Printed in Bend, Oregon

Author: Bill Mason
Editor: David Banks
Cover Design: Lynn Perrault, David Banks
Maps: Bill Mason, Lynn Perrault
Front Cover Photo: Steve Bly
Back Cover Photos: Steve Bly, Brad Teel

This guide is dedicated to my loving wife Jane, my son Hank and, as of this writing, the little person who will soon be my new daughter. With these people in my life, pursuing rising trout has become less important than it once was. My family has made me more fully aware that there is a great deal more to life than fly fishing.

VICINITY MAP

REFERENCED-
STREAMS, LAKES & RESERVOIRS
NTS

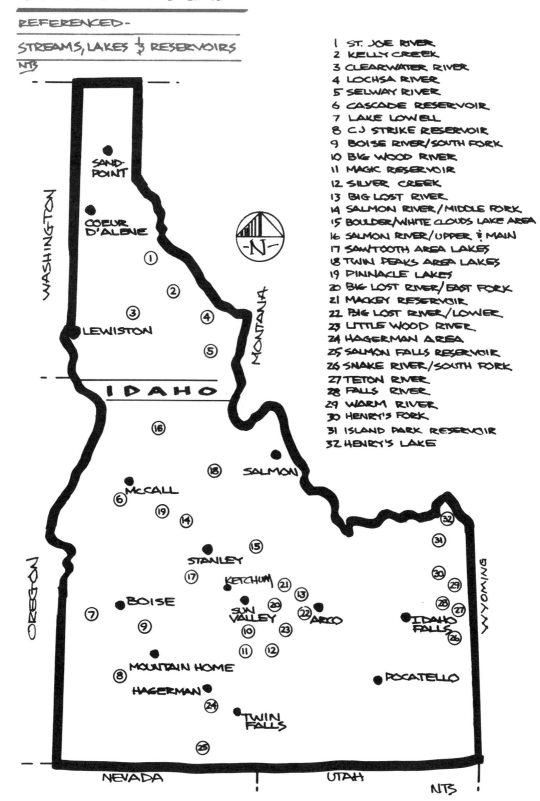

1 ST. JOE RIVER
2 KELLY CREEK
3 CLEARWATER RIVER
4 LOCHSA RIVER
5 SELWAY RIVER
6 CASCADE RESERVOIR
7 LAKE LOWELL
8 CJ STRIKE RESERVOIR
9 BOISE RIVER/SOUTH FORK
10 BIG WOOD RIVER
11 MAGIC RESERVOIR
12 SILVER CREEK
13 BIG LOST RIVER
14 SALMON RIVER/MIDDLE FORK
15 BOULDER/WHITE CLOUDS LAKE AREA
16 SALMON RIVER/UPPER & MAIN
17 SAWTOOTH AREA LAKES
18 TWIN PEAKS AREA LAKES
19 PINNACLE LAKES
20 BIG LOST RIVER/EAST FORK
21 MACKEY RESERVOIR
22 BIG LOST RIVER/LOWER
23 LITTLE WOOD RIVER
24 HAGERMAN AREA
25 SALMON FALLS RESERVOIR
26 SNAKE RIVER/SOUTH FORK
27 TETON RIVER
28 FALLS RIVER
29 WARM RIVER
30 HENRY'S FORK
31 ISLAND PARK RESERVOIR
32 HENRY'S LAKE

WASHINGTON

SAND POINT

COEUR D'ALENE

LEWISTON

MONTANA

IDAHO

SALMON

McCALL

STANLEY

KETCHUM

BOISE

SUN VALLEY

ARCO

IDAHO FALLS

WYOMING

MOUNTAIN HOME

HAGERMAN

POCATELLO

TWIN FALLS

OREGON

NEVADA

UTAH

NTS

Contents

SECTION I
Selected Rivers & Streams

SECTION II
Selected Lakes & Reservoirs

Guidelines

Two points must be made before I mention some general guidelines that relate to this guide. First, I've been totally honest about each body of water in this guide. If my experience is limited or when I relied on information from others, I've mentioned it. Secondly, because conditions change, one should keep in mind this book is a *guide* and not the last word.

Information. No matter where you go fly fishing in Idaho, get information from people who regularly fish that area. Their knowledge, combined with the essential information here, can help you maximize your fly fishing experience. Many reliable sources of this type of local information are listed in the back section of this guide. An area fly shop is your best spot for local information.

Regulations. In this guide I've noted some of Idaho's fishing regulations, especially the well known ones that pertain to a particular water. But because these regulations change from time to time, be sure to always check current state regulations before you head off fishing. The annual *Idaho General Fishing Seasons and Rules* is available at fly shops, sporting goods stores and other outlets or from the Idaho Department of Fish and Game. I suggest you get a copy and review it. And don't forget a fishing license!

Ratings. Each body of water in the main section of this guide has been rated on a scale from 1 to 10. A "10" is the best overall fly fishing water Idaho has to offer. A "1" is fishable, but not much else. The ratings are based on *my* experience, which may not coincide with the experience of others. Therefore, the ratings should be used as a general comparison of fly fishing waters and as a way for you to compare your opinion to mine.

Hatches. It is not the intention of this guide to be a "hatch book". But aquatic insects that are of interest to trout are one of Bill Mason's strong suits. Therefore, hatches that occur on some of the more popular fly fishing waters in Idaho are presented under the heading *Known Hatches*. The important word here is *known*. When key hatches are known they are presented with detailed hatch charts or given brief notice. When there is insufficient hatch information the heading is eliminated. One can also infer some of the insect activity on a particular water based on the fly patterns listed under the *Flies to Use* heading.

Words. This is a "no nonsense" guide. I've tried to avoid a lot of small talk and extraneous detail and what the original no nonsense author Harry Teel (fly fishing guide to Oregon) calls "unimportant falderal". I've provided essential and basic information that will help you select a fly fishing water in Idaho, know what to take and what to expect. As a result you should, in a short amount of time, have a better chance of success when fly fishing in Idaho.

Fly Fishing in Idaho

Some Thoughts on Regulations, Fish and Water

While each fly fishing water in Idaho has its own particular set of blueprints that dictate how it functions, there are also some general characteristics (some man made and some created by nature) that tell us where, when and even how to approach most of the angling in Idaho.

Idaho, and some other western states, now lead most of the country in restrictive or catch & release regulations, something I did not think I would say or write in my lifetime. This helps insure good populations of quality fish now and for the future. Filling a creel with fish depletes the resource, is unproductive, out dated, and is now recognized by many as a poor management tool.

Speaking of fish, years ago the dominate specie of trout in Idaho was the cutthroat. By the turn of this century the rainbow and to a lesser degree brook trout, were added to many fisheries. Later, because of poor water quality, fishing pressure and general degradation the brown trout was added to many waters. Today a major effort to retain the cutthroat in Idaho is underway. For fly fishers, "cutts" as well as the rainbow and browns are the state's primary game fish.

As good as Idaho's regulations are however, it's the water the fish inhabit that make all the great fly fishing work. In Idaho water and fly fishing can be divided into two basic regions, north and south. Most (but not all!) of the best fishing is located in the southern half of the state. Northern waters generally lack good levels of alkalinity necessary to produce strong aquatic insect populations and, in turn, fast growth and large fish. But believe me, you will find enjoyable fly fishing in Northern Idaho. This guide will show you the best waters and when to fish them.

Idaho's water, in one form or another, comes from winter snowpack. When this snow melts in the spring and early summer, many rivers and streams become high, off color, and unfishable. Fly fishers making travel plans for Idaho should take this into consideration. One should always seek stream or lake information from a local source or fly shop.

I maintain that one of Idaho's most precious resource is this water. To satisfy the needs of the state's major economic interest (agriculture) much of this water has been harnessed by dams which provide power and irrigation for farmlands. These impoundments often dictate where and when we fish Idaho's storied rivers and lakes. I find the whole system of Idaho's hydroelectric/irrigation projects a double sided coin. One side of the coin is the fact that Idaho's dams do a good job of controlling runoff. These projects can provide very good early season fishing on rivers that otherwise would be swollen with spring snowmelt. The Henry's Fork is a good example. Stream damage from runoff is also minimized by the controlled releases.

The flip side to this coin is the dry season when irrigation water is needed. Out-flow water levels can be either high or go up and down like a yo-yo. Both can be detrimental to the fishing, and in some cases to the angler. Wading can be difficult if not impossible and a boat may be the only means of access. It is not until the storage of next year's irrigation water begins that water levels become prime. Taking all this into consideration, fall fishing in Idaho can be nothing short of spectacular.

Approximately 68% of Idaho land is government owned. Access to water on most of this land is good. The 32% which is private property along waterways can present fly fishers problems with access. But by Idaho law entire river systems are not private. If the stream is navigable, which is almost everything within reason, the state not only owns that water, but the stream bed up to the mean high water mark. Therefore, once access has been completed, unless by trespass, you are well within your rights to move about or float the waters unrestricted, excluding private property. It's always best to check first.

Idaho is one of the last frontiers for quality "Western-type" angling in this country. Idaho Fish and Game is setting aside more and more quality water and water users are managing the resource better. As a result, Idaho fly fishing will not only be maintained but improved for future generations. But we still need your help. Respect the water systems, your fellow angler and the bounty that lives in Idaho's rivers, streams, lakes and reservoirs. Releasing fish to be caught and enjoyed for another day is still one of our best hopes. Won't you consider these guidelines when fly fishing in Idaho, or anywhere else for that matter:

- Abide by the laws
- Respect property rights
- Never crowd in on another fisher
- Catch and release
- Carry out your litter

Preface

Throughout most of my adult life, I have been the envy of many people, for most think I've had the perfect job. Not only have I taught thousands to cast and fly fish, I have done so on some of the great river systems in Idaho and throughout the world. Not every day of this work has been rosy, and at times my career has been financially frightening. But I must admit that, for twenty-five years, my job has been more satisfying than most conventional occupations.

During this career, I've averaged more than 150 fly fishing days a year on various bodies of water, primarily in Idaho. Even with all that angling time, no fly fisher (self included) is going to know *everything* about every stream or lake in a region as large as an entire state. Plus, it's inevitable that some people will disagree with my rankings, opinions or some aspect of this guide. (I have yet to see the day when fly fishers agree on much of anything.) I'm sure this guide will cause some controversy, disagreement and perhaps some spirited conversation. This is fine. Everyone can have an experience and opinion about fly fishing in Idaho.

Assembling this guide has been a fun way for me to review my experiences and home-state waters. I sincerely hope it helps the out-of-state angler wishing to fish Idaho. And I hope this guide is of use to the many fly fishing Idahoans who need a little help getting around their state. Finally, fly fishing Idaho can be a magnificent experience, and my hope is that this guide adds to the splendor.

Idaho Fly Fishing
Conditions By The Month

Here are general conditions for fly fishing waters in Idaho by month. Use this to help plan your Idaho fly fishing vacation. Or, if you're in the state, a quick glance at this listing will show you where to fish, given the time of year. Water systems are not listed in order of importance. Note: Fishable = Fishable but inconsistent day to day, WD = Weather Dependant. Always consult Idaho fishing regulations and an area fly shop for current information.

January - April

Big Wood River (Prime, WD)
South Fork of the Snake (Prime, WD)
Silver Creek (Good, WD)
South Fork of the Boise (Prime, WD)

Hagerman Area (Prime)
Henry's Fork, Sealy's Area (Prime, WD)
Big Lost Reservoir (Prime, WD)
Lochsa River (Prime, WD)

April - June

Hagerman Area (Prime)
Little Wood River (Prime)
Lake Lowell (Prime)

Main Salmon, Stanley Area, Steelhead, (Prime)
C.J. Strike Reservoir/Bruneau Sand Dunes (Prime)

June - July 10

Silver Creek (Fishable)
Big Wood River (Marginal)
Hagerman Area (Fishable)
Henry's Lake (Fishable)
Henry's Fork at Sealy's (Prime)
Henry's Fork, Warm River to Ashton (Prime)
Henry's Fork, Woodroad 16 (Prime)
Henry's Fork, Box Canyon (Prime)
Lake Lowell (Good - Fishable)
C.J. Strike/Bruneau Sand Dunes (Good)

Kelley Creek (Marginal)
Lochsa River (Marginal)
South Fork of Snake (Marginal)
St. Joe River (Marginal)
Teton Canyon (Good)
Mackey Reservoir (Prime)
South Fork of the Boise (Good - Fishable)
Middle Fork of the Salmon (Marginal - Fishable)
Henry's Fork at Harriman State Park, opens 6/15, (Prime)

July 10 - August 1

Silver Creek (Good plus)
Big Wood River (Prime)
East Fork of Big Lost (Prime if fishing)
Middle Fork of the Salmon (Prime)
South Fork of the Snake (Good)
South Fork of the Boise (Good)
Henry's Lake (Prime)
Henry's Fork, Warm River to Ashton (Good)
Henry's Fork, Harriman State Park (Prime)

Henry's Fork Woodroad Sixteen (Good)
Falls River (Prime)
Salmon River, trout (Fishable)
Warm River (Good)
Kelley Creek (Fishable to Good)
Lochsa River (Fishable - Good)
High Lakes (Good, WD)
St. Joe River (OK - Good)
Teton River (Prime)
Selway River (Fishable - Good)

Continued on page xii.

Idaho Fly Fishing
Conditions By The Month
(continued)

August - September 1

Silver Creek (Prime)
Big Wood River (Good to Prime)
South Fork of Snake (Good)
South Fork of Boise (Good)
Middle Fork of Salmon (Prime)
All High Lakes (Prime)
Henry's Lake (Good)
Henry's Fork Harriman Park (Good)
Lochsa River (Prime)
Henry's Fork Woodroad Sixteen (Fishable)
Henry's Fork, Warm River to Ashton (Good)

Kelley Creek (Prime)
Robinson Creek (Good)
Island Park Reservoir (Good)
St. Joe River (Good to Prime)
Clearwater River, Steelhead (Fishable)
Salmon River, Trout (Fishable)
C.J. Strike/Bruneau (Fishable)
Teton River (Good)
Mackey Reservoir (Fishable)
Selway River (Prime)

September 1- October 1

Silver Creek (Prime)
Big Wood River (Prime)
South Fork of Snake (Prime)
Big Lost River, lower (Prime)
South Fork of Boise (Prime)
Henry's Fork, Sealy's (Prime)
Henry's Fork, Warm River (Fishable)
Henry's Fork, Box Canyon (Good)
Henry's Fork, Woodroad 16 (Good)
Henry Lake (Prime)
Kelley Creek (Prime)

Lochsa River (Prime)
Salmon, Middle Fork (WD, Good)
Salmon by Riggins, Steelhead (Fishable)
Clearwater, Steelhead (Prime)
St. Joe River (Prime)
All High Lakes (Prime, WD)
Teton Lake (Prime)
Henry's Fork, Harriman Park, 9/12 on, (Good)
Selway River (Prime, WD)
Mackey Reservoir (Good)

October - November 30
(snow can be a problem)

Silver Creek (Prime)
Big Wood River (Prime)
South Fork of Snake (Prime)
South Fork of Boise (Prime)
Hagerman Area (Good)
Clearwater River (Fishable - Good)
Lochsa River (Prime)
Henry's Fork at Sealy's (Prime)

Henry's Fork Upper Ranch (Prime)
Henry's Fork Box Canyon (Prime)
Henry's Fork at Box Canyon (Prime)
Little Wood River (Prime)
Big Lost River, Below Mackey Reservoir (Prime)
Main Salmon, Riggins to City of Salmon, Steelhead (Prime)

November 30 - December 31
(Can be very cold, and weather dependent.)

Big Wood River (Good)
Hagerman Area (Good)

South Fork of the Boise (Prime)

SECTION I
Selected
Rivers & Streams

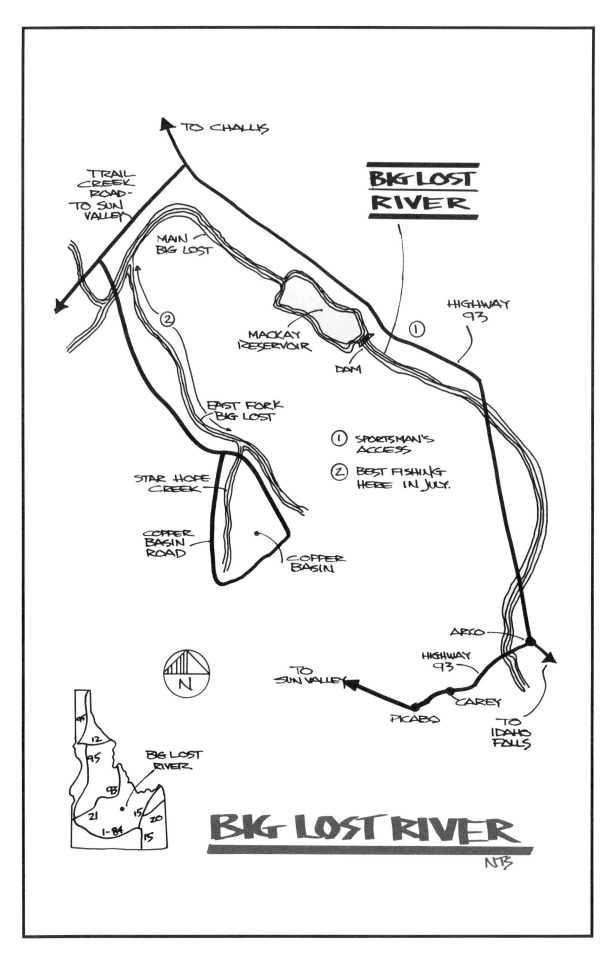

TO CHALLIS

BIG LOST
RIVER

TRAIL
CREEK
ROAD-
TO SUN
VALLEY

MAIN
BIG LOST

MACKAY
RESERVOIR

HIGHWAY
93

DAM

② ①

EAST FORK
BIG LOST

① SPORTSMAN'S
ACCESS

② BEST FISHING
HERE IN JULY.

STAR HOPE
CREEK

COPPER
BASIN
ROAD

COPPER
BASIN

N

ARCO

HIGHWAY
93

TO
SUN VALLEY

CAREY

PICABO

TO
IDAHO
FALLS

BIG LOST
RIVER

49
12
95
93
21   15   20
1-84   15

BIG LOST RIVER
NB

The Big Lost River

*L*ocated 30 miles east of Sun Valley, the Big Lost is a very wadable river that's surrounded by the scenic mountain beauty of two National Forests. This fishery has great quantities of mayflies, caddis and stoneflies. All in all, fly fishing can be a very pleasurable experience here.

In July, the best fly fishing sections are actually the East Fork of the Big Lost or Copper Basin, and the Big Lost below Mackay Reservoir. The water in between is marginal, with the exception of the reservoir (see Comments On Other Lakes & Reservoirs, page 40). Irrigation demands inhibit fish migration and vary water levels affecting fishing and wading. When conditions are right though, fly fishing can be fabulous. In July take along some mosquito repellent.

To reach these waters from Sun Valley/Ketchum, travel over the Trail Creek Summit about 30 miles to Copper Basin road, turn right and follow it to the East Fork. To get to the lower Big Lost, stay on Highway 93 going south past Mackay Reservoir. Look for the Sportsman's Access signs along the road. Take Highway 93 north if coming from Arco and the southeastern reaches of Idaho.

Type of Fish

Primarily rainbow with some cutthroat and cutbows in the upper section and some brook trout in the East Fork.

Known Hatches

Mayflies
Early July: Green Drake (Drunella, doddsi), Western Quill Gordon (Epeorus, longimanus).
July: Cream Dun (Epeorus decptivus), Pink Dun (Heptagenia, elegantula), Blue Winged Olive (Baetis).

Caddis
July: Spotted Caddis (Hydropsyce), Horned Caddis (Oecctis), Tan Caddis (Glossosoma), Micro Caddis (Hydroptila).

Stoneflies
Early July: Golden Stone (Calineuri), Small Yellow Stone (Isoperla and Isogenus), Tan Caddis.

Equipment to Use

Rods: 5 to 6 weight, 8 1/2' to 9'.
Line: Floating line to match rod weight.
Leaders: 4x to 6x, 9'.
Reels: Palm or mechanical drag.
Wading: Chest-high neoprene waders with felt-soled wading shoes. In low water during warm weather the East Fork can be wet-waded. In high water, wading can be treacherous below Mackay Reservoir.

Flies to Use

General Use
Dry patterns: Parachute Adams #12-22, Olive/Yellow Stimulator #10-14, Golden Stone #8, Elk Hair Caddis #14-18, Henryville Caddis #14-18, Rusty Spinner #16-18.
Nymphs: Beaded Prince, Hares Ear #10-16, Brown Flashback #10-16, Black/Olive Wooly Bugger #8-12.

July
Dry patterns: Green Drake #10-12, Mason Green Drake, Gray Wulff, Green Drake #10, Western Quill Gordon #14,

Parachute Adams, Mason Western Quill #14, Cul-De-Canard (C.D.C.) Rusty Spinner #16-18. Golden Stone #8, Small Yellow Stones #12, Madam X, Henry's Fork Golden Stone #8, Small Yellow Stone, Yellow Stone, Yellow Elk Hair Caddis #12, Henryville Caddis, Hemingway Caddis, Kings River Caddis, Elk hair Caddis #14-18.
Nymphs: Flashback #10.

September
Dry patterns: (lower river) Blue Winged Olive #22, Little Olive Parachute #22, Little Chocolate Dun #16, Brown Parachute, Adams Parachute #16.
Nymphs: Beaded Prince, Hares Ear #12-16, Brown Flashback #10-16.

Winter
Dry patterns: (lower river) Add Parachute Adams #20, Beaded Prince, Brown Flashback #10-16, Brassies, Midge pupa and adult #16-20 to the September selections.

When to Fish

On the lower river, if it is fishing, July is the best time. In general, fly fish "The Lost" spring to fall. Check fly shops in Sun Valley and Ketchum for the status of the East Fork.

Season & Limits

Memorial weekend - March 31st. East Fork, 2 fish, none under 14". Winter is whitefish-only season and all trout must be released. Refer to the Idaho Fish and Game regulations booklet.

Accommodation & Services

There are some campgrounds in the region. Hotels, motels, service stations, grocery stores and other services can be found in Sun Valley, Ketchum, Arco and Mackay.

Rating

In February and March the lower section is a 10. Because the East Fork can be inconsistent and high water limits fishing in the lower section most of the summer, overall a 6.5.

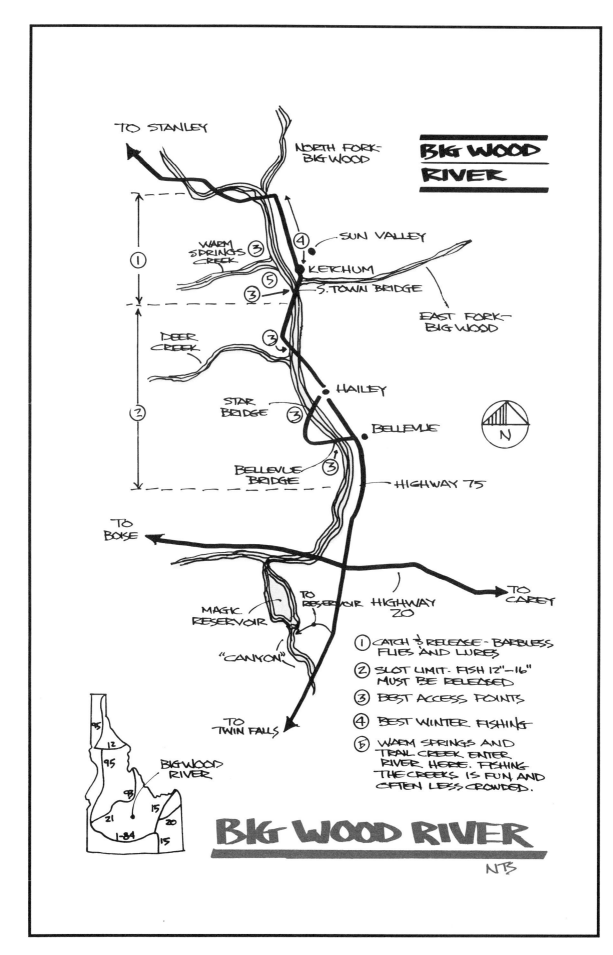

TO STANLEY

NORTH FORK- BIG WOOD

BIG WOOD RIVER

WARM SPRINGS CREEK ③

④ • SUN VALLEY

⑤ • KETCHUM

③ → S. TOWN BRIDGE

EAST FORK- BIG WOOD

DEER CREEK

③

STAR BRIDGE ③

• HAILEY

• BELLEVUE

N

BELLEVUE BRIDGE ③

HIGHWAY 75

TO BOISE

TO RESERVOIR HIGHWAY 20

TO CAREY

MAGIC RESERVOIR

"CANYON"

① CATCH & RELEASE - BARBLESS FLIES AND LURES

② SLOT LIMIT- FISH 12"-16" MUST BE RELEASED

③ BEST ACCESS POINTS

④ BEST WINTER FISHING

⑤ WARM SPRINGS AND TRAIL CREEK ENTER RIVER HERE. FISHING THE CREEKS IS FUN, AND OFTEN LESS CROWDED.

TO TWIN FALLS

95 / 12 / 95 / 93 / 15 / 21 / I-84 / 20 / 15

BIG WOOD RIVER

BIG WOOD RIVER

NB

The Big Wood River

A rich, freestone-type stream, the Big Wood River flows through the Wood River Valley in the Ketchum/Sun Valley area. Trout of high quality and good size challenge fly fishers most of the entire 75 miles of the Wood.

The most popular fishing area is from the town of Bellevue north to the North Fork of the Big Wood River. The section below Magic Reservoir or "The Canyon" is good yet mystifying. Fall irrigation storage reduces the water flow to a mere trickle but surprisingly, heavy fish kills do not result.

The Big Wood can be accessed from many points off Highway 75 between Sun Valley (north) and Bellevue (south). Access to "The Canyon" is off Highway 75 on the road to Magic dam. Much of the river is bordered with private property which limits entry. Always check at a fly shop or ask permission. Once on the river, travel in the high water mark is unrestricted.

Type of Fish

Rainbow trout.

Known Hatches

The Big Wood River's hatches are presented on page 51.
Early July: Green Drake (Drunella), Western Quill Gordon (Epeorus), Golden Stone (Calineuri), Small Yellow Stone (Isoperla).
July-August: Spotted Caddis (Hydropsyce), Horned Caddis (Oecctis), Tan Caddis (Glossosoma), Micro Caddis (Hydroptila), Cream Dun (Epeorus), Pink Dun (Heptagenia).
July-October: Blue Winged Olive (Baetis).
August-September: Western March Brown (Rithrogena), Red Quill Gordon (Timpanoga).
September-October: Chocolate Dun (Serratella).

Equipment to Use

Rods: 5 to 6 weight, 8 1/2' to 9'.
Lines: Floating lines matched to rod weight.
Leaders: 4x to 7x, 9' to 12'.
Reel: Palm drag.
Wading: In low water during warm weather, wading shoes and shorts are fine. In high water use chest-high neoprene waders and felt-soled shoes for greater maneuverability.

Flies to Use

General Use
Dry patterns: Parachute Adams #12-22, Olive/Yellow Stimulator #10-14, Golden Stone #8, Elk Hair Caddis #14-18, Henryville Caddis #14-18, Rusty Spinner #16-18.
Nymphs: Beaded Prince, Hares Ear #10-16, Brown Flashback #10-16, Black/Olive Wooly Bugger #8-12.

July
Dry patterns: Green Drake #10-12, Mason Green Drake, Gray Wulff, Green Drake, Western Quill Gordon #14, Parachute Adams, Mason Western Quill, Cul-De-Canard (C.D.C.) Rusty spinner #16-18. Golden Stone #8, Small Yellow Stones #12, Madam X, Henry's Fork Golden Stone #8, Small Yellow Stone, Yellow Elk Hair Caddis #12, Henryville Caddis, Hemingway Caddis, Kings River Caddis, Elk Hair Caddis #14-18.

Nymphs: Beaded and regular Flashback #10, Hare's Ear, Prince #10-14.

August
Dry patterns: Blue Wing Olives #22, Olive Parachute, Adams Parachute #18, Cream Dun #16, Parachute Pale Morning Dun, Little Cahill #16, C.D.C. Rusty spinner #16-18, Pinkish Dun #16-14, Parachute Light Cahill, Pink Albert #16, Western March Brown #14-16, Tan Parachute #14-16.

September
Dry patterns: Great Red Quills #10-12, Mason Red Quill, Gray Wulff #10, Blue Winged Olive, Little Olive Parachute, Little Chocolate Dun #16, Brown Parachute, Adams Parachute #10-12.
Nymphs: Beaded Prince, Hares Ear #12-16, Midge Pupa #16-18.

Winter
Add Parachute Adams #20, Beaded Prince, Hare's Ear #12-16, Brassies, White Midge Pupa #18-20 to the above selection.

When to Fish

July through October the upper section near Sun Valley is excellent. Winter fishing here can be good. August through October is the best time to fish the lower section. Entering the Big Wood River in Ketchum are Trail Creek and Warm Springs, small creeks that can provide some very fun fly fishing.

Seasons & Limits

General season, restricted seasons, slot limits and catch and release sections vary. Consult the Idaho Fish & Game regulation booklet.

Accommodations and Services

Sun Valley, a major international resort, and Ketchum have an endless offering of accommodations, food and services at all price ranges. Camping is available at the Forest Service Campground 10 miles north of Ketchum. R.V. hook-ups are available 1 mile south of Ketchum.

Rating

The Big Wood is just a great trout stream, a solid 9.

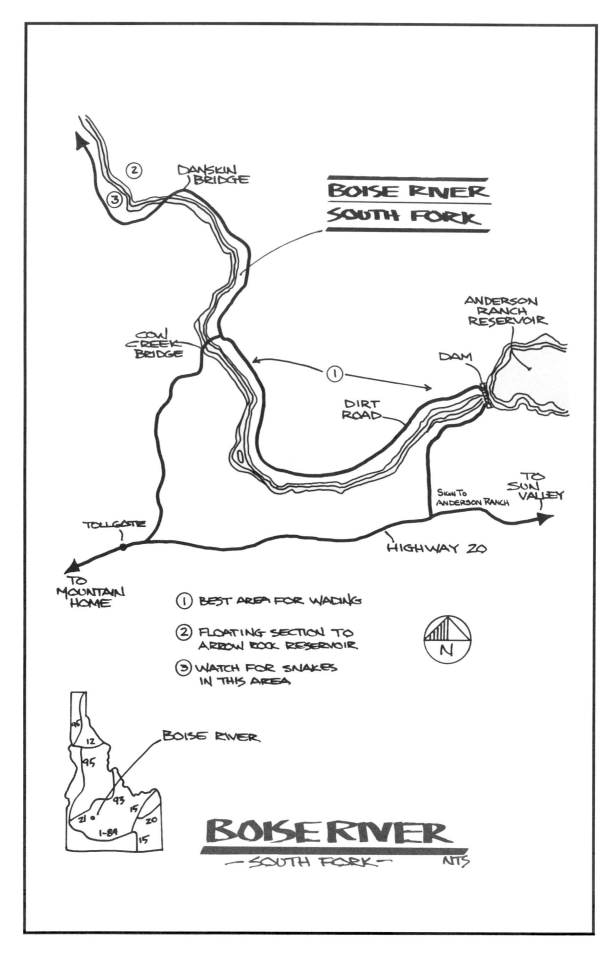

BOISE RIVER
SOUTH FORK

① BEST AREA FOR WADING

② FLOATING SECTION TO ARROW ROCK RESERVOIR

③ WATCH FOR SNAKES IN THIS AREA

BOISE RIVER
—SOUTH FORK—   NTS

The Boise River South Fork

Residents of Central and Southwestern Idaho are fortunate to be so close to one of the state's best trout streams. It's not uncommon for business people from Boise to leave work and, in about an hour, get into some great fly fishing.

The South Fork of the Boise, located east of Boise and north of Mountain Home, is a medium sized freestone stream of high alkalinity and diverse and heavy aquatic insect populations. The upper section that flows into the reservoir has small trout and is not often fished. The major fly fishing action is on the two main sections below Anderson Ranch dam.

The first section, 12 miles below the dam, is picturesque river canyon that is easily accessed by road, and hence, most often fished. Most of the 30 miles of the second section below Danskin Bridge, is accessible only by boat or raft. This part of the river, called "rattlesnake gulch" by locals, demands a cautious eye for snakes. The river requires skilled boating technique.

The quick route to the river is out of Mountain Home. Go 20 miles north on Highway 20 where you'll see signs announcing "Anderson Ranch Dam" and Dixi. Take Dixi road down hill to the dam crossing and to where river access begins. Down stream about 10 miles is Cow Creek Bridge where a good dirt road provides access and entry to and from the river and connections to Highway 20.

Type of Fish

A wild rainbow trout fishery.

Known Hatches

Mayflies
August-September: Blue Winged Olive (Baetis, bicaudatus).
August-September: Pink Alberts (Epeorus, albertea).
September-October: Blue Winged Olive (Baetis, tricaudatus).

Stoneflies
July-August: Little Yellow Stone (Isoperla, Isogenus), Lime Sally (Alloperla).
March: Early Brown Stone (Brachyptepa).

Equipment to Use

Rods: 5 to 6 weight, 8 1/2' to 9 1/2'.
Lines: Floating lines matched to rod weight.
Leaders: 4x to 7x, 9' to 12'.
Reel: Mechanical or palm drag.
Wading: In low water, chest-high neoprene waders and felt-soled shoes. In high water, chest-high neoprene waders and felt-soled shoes, stream cleats and a wading staff.

Flies to Use

Dry Patterns: (high water) Olive/tan, Elk Hair Caddis, Hemingway Caddis, Goddard Caddis #12-16. (low water) Partridge, black, brown Kings River #14-18. Soft hackle patterns in the pupa stage. Little Yellow Stone, Lime Sally, Early Brown Stone, Yellow Partridge #12-16. Blue Wing Olive #20, Pink Albert #14-16, Slate/Tan No Hackle.

Seasons & Limits

Special Regulation: Artificial flies and lures, 2 fish limit none between 12 and 20 inches. Winter whitefish season, trout must be released. See the Idaho Department of Fish and Game for exact seasons and limits.

When to Fish

Around Labor Day when water storage for the following year begins, the river level drops and the fabulous fly fishing begins. Most of the best fishing is from the dam to Cow Creek Bridge. The Cow Creek to Danskin stretch is also good.

Accommodations & Service

Limited campsites are available at Anderson Ranch reservoir. Many motels and services in the city of Mountain Home.

Rating

In high water, a 7. In low water the rating quickly moves to a 9.5.

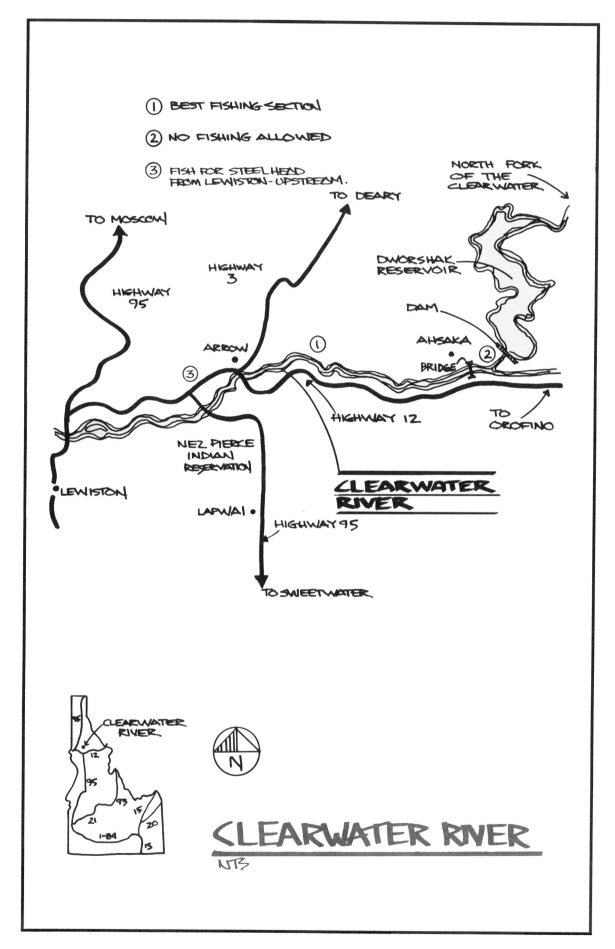

① BEST FISHING SECTION

② NO FISHING ALLOWED

③ FISH FOR STEELHEAD FROM LEWISTON-UPSTREAM.

TO DEARY

NORTH FORK OF THE CLEARWATER

TO MOSCOW

HIGHWAY 3

HIGHWAY 95

DWORSHAK RESERVOIR

DAM

ARROW

AHSAKA

BRIDGE

②

①

③

TO OROFINO

HIGHWAY 12

NEZ PIERCE INDIAN RESERVATION

CLEARWATER RIVER

●LEWISTON

LAPWAI ●

HIGHWAY 95

TO SWEETWATER

CLEARWATER RIVER

CLEARWATER RIVER
NTS

N

The Clearwater River

*T*he Clearwater has long been considered Idaho's top steelhead river boasting a strain of these fish that can exceed 20 pounds. These "B" run fish (versus the smaller "A" run) enter the Columbia River August 25th after spending two or three years in the ocean. They return as brutes in good condition and are much more active than the steelhead that remain over the winter months and are fished in the spring. Look for steelhead in the lower 1/3 of pools and runs especially above heavy riffles and whitewater.

Clearwater River trout populations tend to be slim or limited. But if trout is your game, you will find some cutthroat and steelhead smolts.

Type of Fish

Primarily steelhead and smolts with some cutthroat and bass in the lower sections.

Equipment to Use

Steelhead
Rods: 8 or 9 weight, 9'.
Line: Floating or sink tip to match rod weight.
Leaders: 0x or 1x, 7' - 9'.
Reel: Mechanical drag is best, palm drag will work.
Wading: Chest-high neoprene waders with felt-soled wading shoes.

Trout
Rods: 5 to 6 weight, 7 1/2' to 9'.
Lines: Floating lines matched to rod weight.
Leaders: 4x to 7x, 9' to 12'.
Reel: Palm drag.
Wading: Chest-high neoprene waders and felt soled shoes.

Flies to Use

Steelhead
Green Butted Skunk, Thor, Skykomish Sunrise, Purple Peril, Giant Fall Orange Caddis (wet) and Bucktail Caddis (dry) #4-8. The Bomber series, large Royal Wulff and Grasshopper, skated and twitched on the swing will work. Atlantic salmon Spey-type patterns are also being used here with success.

Trout
Dry Patterns: Royal Wulff, Elk Hair Caddis, Adams, Parachute Adams, Golden Stone #8, Yellow Stimulator #6-8.
Nymphs: Prince, Hares Ear, Brown Stonefly #10-14.

When to Fish

The best steelhead fishing occurs during the catch & release period August 1st to October 15th. Most is done from the city of Lewiston upstream, to Ahsahka Bridge, just downstream of Dworshak Dam. After October 15th it's "catch & keep". Fish for trout all season.

Seasons & Limits

Idaho's steelhead waters have special regulations, seasons, and boundaries. Consult the Idaho Fish and Game regulations booklet for steelhead and trout seasons and limits on the Clearwater.

Accommodations & Services

The cites of Lewiston and Orofino have everything you need.

Rating

If the steelhead run is good an 8, if not, a 3.

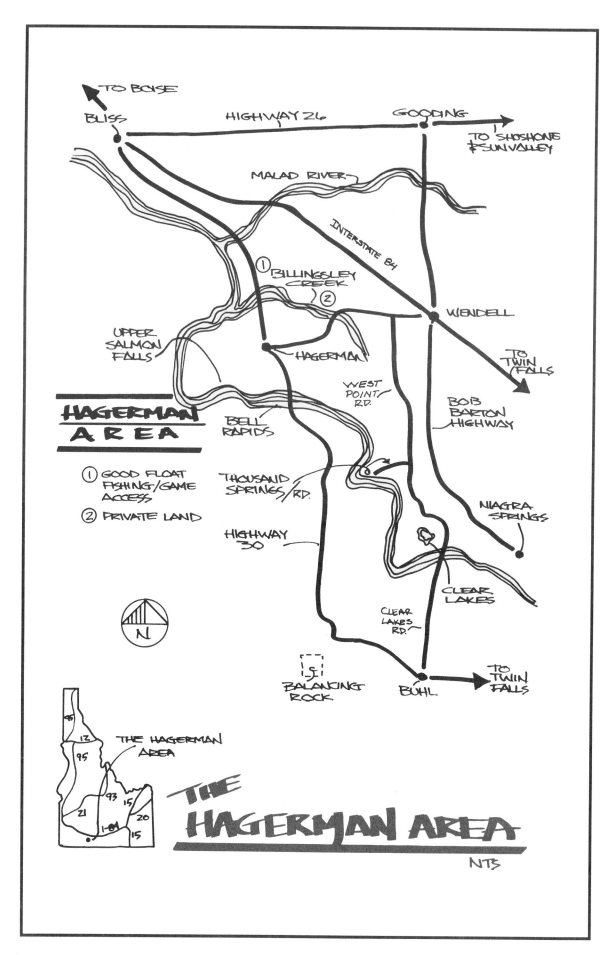

The Hagarman Area

*F*ly fishing in Idaho during April, May and early June can be limited by area closures or unfavorable water conditions. The Hagerman area presents a unique water situation which solves this seasonal dilemma.

Located in the south central part of the state, this area is fed by five major river systems and an aquifer located beneath the upper Snake River plain. After some 4,000 years underground, water gushes forth (in many places) through the walls of the Snake River Canyon between Twin Falls and Hagerman. This pure water is used to produce 95% of the commercially raised trout in the Untied States. The water in Niagara Springs, Thousand Springs, Clear Lakes, Billingsley Creek and the Bell Rapid area on the Snake River provide some very good fly fishing.

These springs contain a fair amount of trout, given their relatively short run into the Snake River. In some stretches the spring water is almost too pure and aquatic insect populations suffer. Trout rarely grow over 16" in this water. In areas that are not entirely spring-fed, larger trout can be found.

The toughest part about fishing this area is finding everything. Traveling the farm roads of southern Idaho is not always easy. These directions will get you as close as any. Use Wendell, Idaho as a starting point and, if all else fails, ask for directions in Simmerly's in Wendell.

Thousand Springs/Clear Lake
Take the main road to Hagerman and turn left on West Point Road (some call it Clear Lakes Road) and go about 4 miles. Before dropping into the Snake River canyon, turn right at Thousand Springs Road. For Clear Lakes, continue on West Point into the Canyon. Clear Lakes is at the canyon base.

Billingsley Creek
Take the main road to Hagerman. At the base of Vader Grade cross Billingsley Creek where access is limited. Or, travel west on Highway 30 from the town of Hagerman. Check in Wendell for access to lower Billingsley.

Bell Rapids
Take Hagerman Road to Highway 30, east of the town of Hagerman. Turn left toward Buhl and go over the bridge crossing the Snake River. Fish downstream of the bridge.

Niagara Springs
Take the Bob Barton Highway (the Main Road) south out of Wendell. Follow the road into the base of Snake River Canyon and look for Niagara.

Type of Fish
Rainbow and a few browns in the Snake River.

Known Hatches

Mayflies
April-May: Blue Wing Olive (Baetis).
June-July: Pale Morning Dun (Ephemerella, inermis).

Equipment to Use
Rods: 4 to 6 weight, 8 1/2' to 9'.
Lines: Floating and sink-tip lines matched to rod weight.
Leaders: 4x to 7x, 9' to 12'.
Reel: Click drag, single action.

Wading: Water is very cold, use chest-high neoprene waders and felt-soled shoes. In the Bell Rapids area above upper Salmon Falls and Clear Lakes use a float tube or boat.

Flies to Use

Spring Creeks
Dry patterns: Baetis #18-22, Brown Caddis #16, Pale Morning Dun Parachute #18-20, Parachute Adams, Olive Dun #18-20, Parachute Pale Morning Dun #16-20, Kings River and Partridge Caddis #14-18.
Nymphs: Pheasant Tail, Brown Flashback #14-18.

Bell Rapids
Wet patterns: Black, Black/Olive and variegated Brown Wooly Buggers #2-8.

Clear Lakes
Wet patterns: Green Damsel, Black and Brown Marabou Leech, Stayner Ducktail #6-10, Fresh Water Shrimp #10-12.

When to Fish
Fish the springs and creeks and Bell rapids in the early spring. Try Clear Lakes in the spring and fall.

Seasons & Limits
The season is generally year-round with a 2 trout limit. Other restrictions and limits may apply or change. Consult the Idaho Department of Fish and Game regulations booklet for complete area information.

Accommodations & Services
Motels in Wendell and Buhl. Restaurants in Hagerman.

Rating
If the spring creeks had bigger fish the rating would be quite high. As it is, a 6.5.

Henry's Fork of the Snake River • Hatch Chart

SECTION	HATCH	STAGE/ TIME OF DAY	FEB	MAR	APR	MAY	JUN	JULY	AUG	SEPT	OCT	NOV
1,2,4,5	Baetis sp. (Blue Winged Olive)	D, pm	■	■								
1,2,5	Ephemerella inermis (Pale Morning Dun)	S, am, D, am-pm						■	■			
1,2,5	Drunella (Ephemerella) grandis (Green Drake)	D, pm						■	■			
1,2	Ephemera simulans (Brown Drake)	D, S, eve					■					
5	Siphlonurus occidentalis (Gray Drake)	S, eve								■		
1,2,5	Drunella (Ephemerella) flavilinea (Leadwing Olive)	D, pm S, eve						■	■			
1,2	Baetis (Pseudocloeon) edmundsi (Bright Olive Dun)	D, pm							■			
1	Tricorythodes minutus (Trico)	S, am							■	■		
1	Callibaetis nigritus (Speckled Spinner)	S, am							■	■		
1,2,5	Paraleptophlebia debilis (Slate Mahogany Dun)	D, pm								■	■	
1,2,5	Baetis tricaudatus (Blue Wing Olive)	D, pm								■		
3,4,5,6	Stoneflies Pteronarcys sp. (Salmon Fly)	pm					■	■				
3,4,6	Acroneuria sp. (Golden Stone)	pm						■	■			
3,4,6	Isogenus sp. (Small Yellow Stone)	pm						■	■			
2,3,4,5,6	Caddis Various sp.	all day		■		■	■	■				

S = Spinner Stage
D = Dun Stage

am = Sunrise to Noon
pm = Noon - 6 p.m.
eve = Evening

1. Harriman St. Park
3. Riverside/ Warm River
5. Sealey's

2. Osborn/Riverside
4. Warm River/Ashton
6. Box Canyon

Henry's Fork
Of The Snake River

*I*n the last 20 years Henry's Fork notoriety has reached every corner of the fly fishing world. Located in the upper northeast part of Idaho, "The Fork" provides some 50 miles of the most complex fly fishing river system in the West. Highway 191 leading to Yellowstone National Park is the main corridor.

This river will always have a very special place in my heart. It was on this river, some 25 years ago that I started, learned and applied my professional career. In these early years, with the river almost to myself, I helped discover insect hatches and develop many fly patterns for the river. Ah, for those times again.

Probably the peak fly fishing years on "The Fork" were from 1970 to the mid 1980's. In the late 80's a sharp decline in fish population occurred. Mike Lawson, owner of Henry's Fork Anglers and present "Dean" of the Henry's Fork explained that, "Many complex and inter-related reasons lead to the rivers recent decline. A recent study showed that during the drought years, siltation occurred, hurting spawning and fry habitat. Normally, this is flushed out in the spring, but because water was stored in Island Park Reservoir during the drought years (1987-1992) this did not happen. This knowledge, and better cooperation among government agencies, means we believe we can restore "The Fork" to its former glory." Present challenges aside, the Henry's Fork is one of the great and classic dry fly streams in the world.

Since it is easier to understand this complicated river section by section, we will depart slightly from our standard format. The basic information needed to fly fish all sections of the Henry's Fork is summarized below. The pages that follow describe each section, starting upstream and moving downstream.

Type of Fish

Primarily rainbow trout with a decent population of brown trout in the lower river from Warm River downstream. Some brook trout can be found in Box Canyon and the upper river.

Known Hatches

The extensive hatches of the Henry's Fork are presented in the hatch chart on the facing page 12. Refer to this chart for each of the river sections that follow.

Equipment to Use

Rods: For flat, smooth water, 3 to 6 weight, 8' to 9'. For casting big dry flies, 6 to 7 weight, 8 1/2' to 9 1/2'. For big weighted nymphs and streamers, 7 to 8 weight, 9' to 9 1/2'.
Line: Floating lines to match rod weight.
Leaders: 4x and 5x, 9' for dry flies. 4x, 7' to 9' with split shot weights and a strike indicator for nymphing.
Reel: Mechanical or palm drag.
Wading: Chest-high neoprene waders with felt-soled shoes. A boat or raft is helpful in most sections. If you are unfamiliar with this section of river or boating in general, consult a qualified guide or outfitter before taking to the river in a boat.

Accommodations & Services

Although small motels are located in St. Anthony and Ashton, most people stay in the Last Chance/Island Park area. Camping is available in Forest Service areas, primarily at Box Canyon. Cabins can be rented at Pond's Lodge and Mack's Inn. Alpenhaus Motel in Last Chance is also convenient. R.V. hook-ups at the K.O.A., Ponds Lodge and McCreas Ranch (off Shotgun Valley Road). Up-scale accommodations (food included) can be found at Elk Creek Ranch, Henry's Fork Lodge and Three Rivers Ranch at Warm River. Restaurants, groceries and gas are readily available.

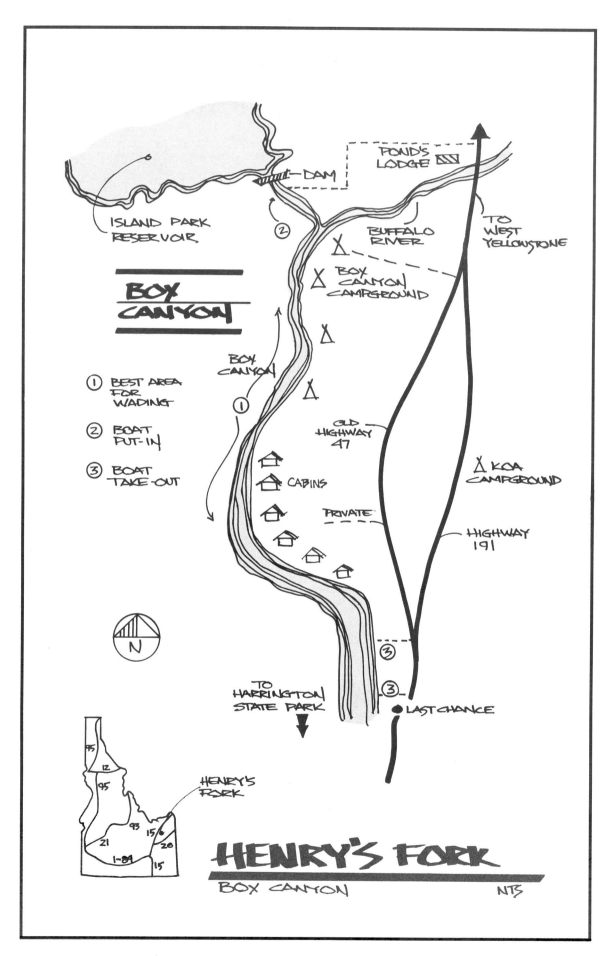

ISLAND PARK
RESERVOIR

DAM

POND'S
LODGE

BUFFALO
RIVER

TO
WEST
YELLOWSTONE

BOX
CANYON

② BOX
CANYON
CAMPGROUND

BOX
CANYON

①

① BEST AREA
FOR
WADING

② BOAT
PUT-IN

③ BOAT
TAKE-OUT

OLD
HIGHWAY
47

KOA
CAMPGROUND

CABINS

PRIVATE

HIGHWAY
191

N

③

③

LAST CHANCE

TO
HARRINGTON
STATE PARK

95
12
95
93
21
15 6
1-84
28
15

HENRY'S
FORK

HENRY'S FORK
BOX CANYON

NTS

The Upper River Section

From the 1920's to the 1950's most people fished the section of the river above Island Park reservoir. Access to Coffee Pot Rapids and Henry's Lake outlet (Mack's Inn area) was convenient. There are nice fish at Coffee Pot rapids and at the famed Quarter Mile Pool below Coffee Pot Lodge, but most tend to be small. Take Highway 191 to Macks Inn and ask for directions for fly fishing this area.

Box Canyon

This canyon, below Island Park dam is quite simply a *gorgeous* place to cast a fly. True monster trout patrol this 3 mile stretch and their presence has enticed fly fishers for years. In this section, one has a reasonable opportunity to take a 10 pound trout on a dry fly, big nymph or streamer, but it's a challenge. This area has fast water, odd shaped boulders and slick rocks, making wading difficult. For this reason many anglers don't fish "The Canyon".

If you are wading this section, take the Old Mesa Scenic Byway (old Highway 47) from Last Chance where various dirt roads, including Box Canyon Campground take you to the canyon rim. If floating, put-in is below Island Park Dam and take-out is at Last Chance.

Type of Fish
Mostly rainbow with some brook trout.

When to Fish
Fish all season for trout in the 8" to 14" range. For larger trout fish June-July 10 and September 20 through October, casting heavily weighted nymphs and sculpin-type streamers. The short-lived Salmon Fly and Golden Stone hatch in June and early July is an excellent time for big fish.

Seasons & Limits
General season, catch and release. Seasons and limits can change, consult the Idaho Fish & Game regulation booklet.

Flies to Use
Box Canyon is paved with Mayflies, Caddis and small Stoneflies. Because of the fast, turbulent water, precise imitations are not needed.

Dry Patterns: Royal Wulff, Humpy, Elk Hair Caddis #14-16, Stimulator #10-14.

Nymphs: Prince #8-12, Flashback, Hare's Ear #10-14.

Salmon Fly hatch: Fish the lower to mid section early-June. Fish the upper section mid-June. Salmon Fly #4-6, Henry's Fork, Bird's Salmon Fly #4-6, Black Rubber Leg Nymph #2-4.

Golden Stone hatch: Usually June 20-July 15. Golden Stone, Salmon Fly tied in Golden Stone colors #6-8, Black Rubber Legs #4-8, Sculpin-type streamers #2-4.

Rating
In June with the Salmon Fly hatch, a 9. Overall a 6.

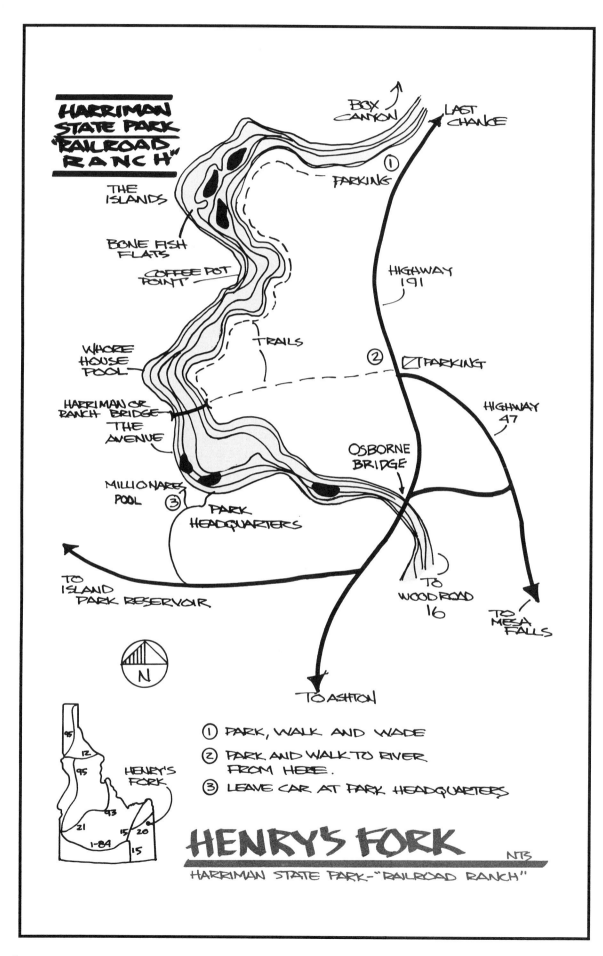

HENRY'S FORK

HARRIMAN STATE PARK - "RAILROAD RANCH"

Harriman State Park / Railroad Ranch

To many fly fishers the 7 miles of river in the Last Chance/Harriman State Park area *IS* the Henry's Fork. Despite problems with siltation, weeds and regulations, this is some of the greatest dry fly water in the Untied States.

Because "The Ranch" (as many locals still call it) is famous, it doesn't mean it's easy to fly fish. Hatches present themselves readily yet don't always indicate what the fish are eating. And, as this arca is a prolific aquatic insect factory, one is continually faced with complex hatch situations. At times as many as five species of mayflies, in various stages, can be on the water at the same time. Add simultaneous caddis activity and things get even more challenging.

To get to this fabled section of water, take Highway 191 north towards Last Chance and look for a turn-off and parking lot to access the upper section. For the middle section, access the river from Middle Ranch Road where Highway 191 and 47 intersect. Park here and walk down to the river. To access the lower section, turn off Highway 191 at Green Canyon Road (near Osborne bridge) and head for the park headquarters.

Walking and wading is the most common way to fish this area with access at the three locations mentioned. Floating and wading is also popular on this section, providing convenient access to all the water. Put-in is at Last Chance near the north end of the park. Take-out is at Osborne Bridge.

Type of Fish
Rainbow trout.

Known Hatches
Refer to the hatch chart on page 12.

Flies to Use

June
Dun hatch mornings, spinner fall late morning/evening.
Dry patterns: Pale Morning Dun #14-20, Gray/Yellow No-Hackle #16-20, Parachute Pale Morning Dun and Thorax #18, Western Green Drake #10, Green Drake Paradun, Crippled Dun Drake.
Nymphs: Crippled Green Drake Dun, Brown Flashback #14-16.

July
E. flavilinea considered best hatch on the Ranch.
Dry patterns: Flav's or Leadwinged Olives #14, Western Slate Olive Dun, Slate/Olive No-Hackle, Olive Parachute #14-16. Brown Drake #10, Paradun Brown Drake, Partridge Brown Drake Spinner, Cul-De-Canard (C.D.C.), Hen Rusty Spinner #14-16, Pale Morning Dun #20.

August
Sporadic mid-month Callibaetis spinner fall in morning, huge late month Baetis hatch.
Dry patterns: Speckled Spinner #14-16, Partridge Spinner, Gray Parachute and Slate/Gray No-Hackle #14-16, Pale Olive Dun #20-22, Pale Olive Parachute #22, Trico or White/Black Spinner #18-20, C.D.C., White/Black Hen Spinner #18-20, Grasshoppers.

September
Afternoon Paraleps emergence mid-month to September.
Dry patterns: Slate Mahogany Dun #16, Slate/Tan and Slate Mahogany No-Hackles, Regular and Parachute Chocolate Duns #16, Fall Blue Winged Olive #20. Gray/Light, Olive No-Hackle or Parachute, slow water Caddis #14-20.
Nymphs: Pheasant Tail, Mason Baetis #18.

Additional notes: 5x tippets are often used here while 6x is common and 7x is getting more popular. Try downstream, drag-free presentations, though some upstream casting can be successful. Caddis activity in this area (and Last Chance) can be heavy, especially in June and July. Also try Terrestrials; Black Ants, Brown Flying Ants, and Black Beetle #14-18.

Seasons & Limits
Consult the Idaho Fish & Game regulation booklet. Generally the Harriman Park northern boundary to Harriman Bridge, from June 15 - November 30, is catch and release, barbless flies only. Harriman Middle Bridge to Osborne, from June 15 - September 30 is catch and release, barbless flies only.

Rating
Years ago, as a classic dry fly stream this area was a 10. As of this writing it is a 5, but when this area "comes back" it will quickly return to a 10.

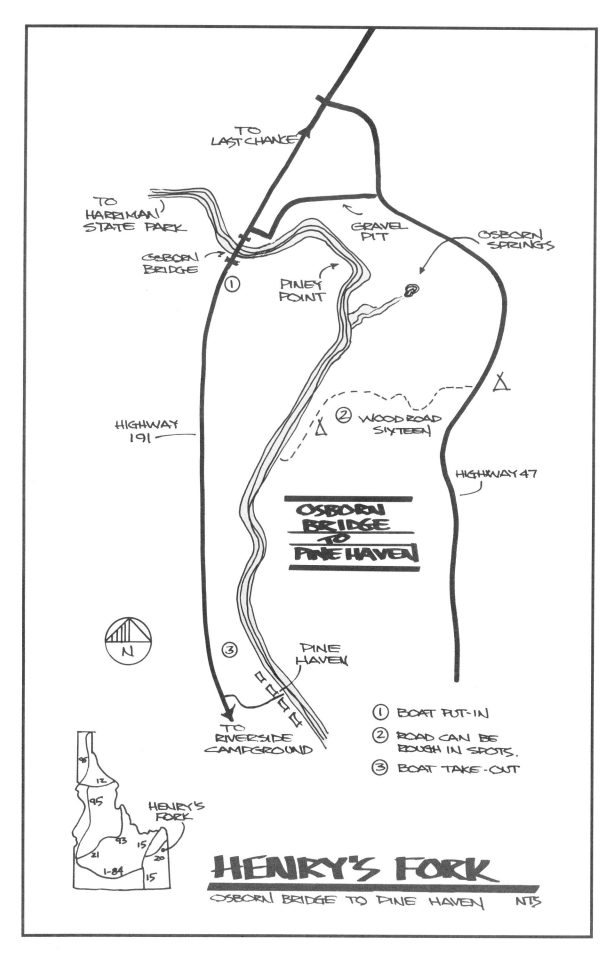

TO
LAST CHANCE

TO
HARRIMAN
STATE PARK

OSBORN
BRIDGE

①

PINEY
POINT

GRAVEL
PIT

OSBORN
SPRINGS

HIGHWAY
191

② WOOD ROAD
SIXTEEN

HIGHWAY 47

OSBORN
BRIDGE
TO
PINE HAVEN

N

③

PINE
HAVEN

TO
RIVERSIDE
CAMPGROUND

① BOAT PUT-IN

② ROAD CAN BE
ROUGH IN SPOTS.

③ BOAT TAKE-OUT

95
12
95
HENRY'S
FORK
93 15
21
20
1-84
15

HENRY'S FORK

OSBORN BRIDGE TO PINE HAVEN   NTS

Osborne Bridge to Pine Haven (Woodroad 16)

Over the years this area has been called the Gravel Pit, Osborne Springs, Piney Point or the most commonly accepted label, Woodroad 16. Though similar in structure to the nearby Harriman State Park section, the slow meandering river runs deep, so crossing can only be made at selected spots. Easy and quick access add to the many positive attributes of this water. To get to the upper section, from Highway 191 go to Osborne Bridge, turn east (downstream) and follow a dirt road to the gravel pit road. Or take the Mesa Falls Scenic Byway (old Highway 47) 2 to 3 miles until a dirt road marked Woodroad 16 heads you toward the river. Woodroad 16 is a rough logging road that, especially when wet, can be an adventure requiring 4 wheel drive in some locations. If you float, put-in at Osborne Bridge, take-out at Pine Haven, a private residential area.

Type of Fish
Rainbow trout.

Flies to Use

June
Dun hatch mornings, spinner fall late morning/evening.
Dry patterns: Pale Morning Dun #14-20, Gray/Yellow No-Hackle #16-20, Parachute Pale Morning Dun and Thorax #18, Western Green Drake #10, Green Drake Paradun #10, Crippled Dun Drake #10.
Nymphs: Crippled Dun Nymph.

July
Dry patterns: Flav's or Leadwinged Olives #14, Western Slate Olive Dun, Slate/Olive No-Hackle or Olive Parachute #14-16, Brown Drake #10, Paradun Brown Drake, Partridge Brown Drake Spinner #10, Cul-De-Canard (C.D.C.) or Hen Rusty Spinner #14-16, Pale Morning Dun #20.

August
Sporadic mid-month Callibaetis spinner fall in morning, huge late month Baetis hatch.
Dry patterns: Speckled Spinner #14-16, Partridge Spinner,

Gray Parachute and Slate/Gray No-Hackle #14-16, Pale Olive Dun #20-22, Pale Olive Parachute #22, Trico or White/Black Spinner #18-20, C.D.C., White/Black Hen Spinner #18-20, Grasshoppers.

September
Afternoon Paraleps emergence mid-month to October.
Dry patterns: Slate Mahogany Dun #16, Slate/Tan and Slate Mahogany No-Hackles, Regular and Parachute Chocolate Duns #16, Fall Blue Winged Olive #20, Gray/light, slow water Olive No-Hackle, Parachute Caddis #14-20.
Nymphs: Pheasant Tail, Mason Baetis #18, slow water Caddis #14-20.
Terrestrials: Black Ants, Brown Flying Ants, Black Beetle #14-18, Grasshoppers.

Seasons & Limits
General season, catch and release. Consult the Idaho Fish & Game regulation booklet.

Rating
In June a solid 8, in other times this section slips to a 5.

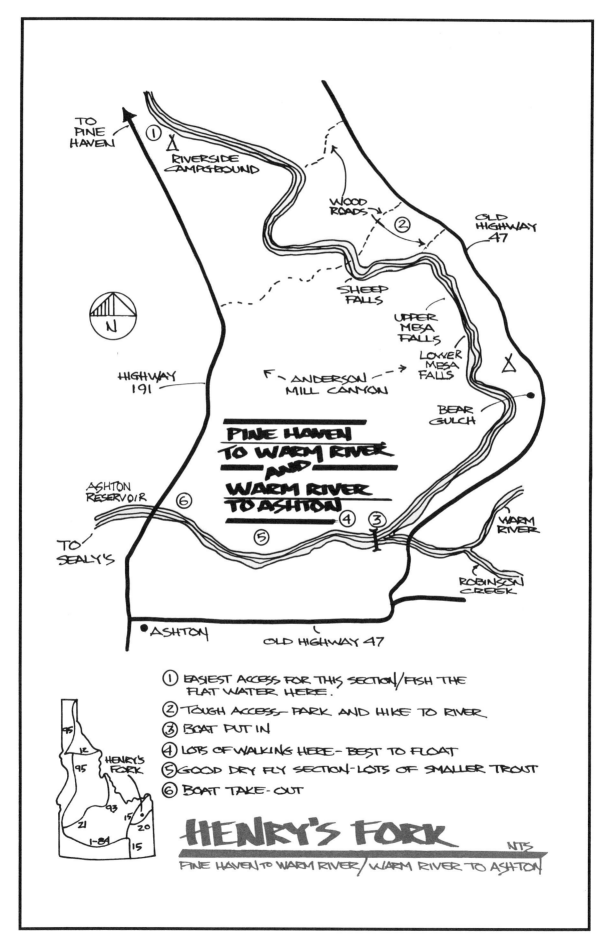

TO PINE HAVEN

① RIVERSIDE CAMPGROUND

WOOD ROADS

②

OLD HIGHWAY 47

SHEEP FALLS

UPPER MESA FALLS

LOWER MESA FALLS

N

HIGHWAY 191

ANDERSON MILL CANYON

BEAR GULCH

PINE HAVEN TO WARM RIVER AND WARM RIVER TO ASHTON

ASHTON RESERVOIR

⑥

④ ③

⑤

WARM RIVER

TO SEALY'S

ROBINSON CREEK

●ASHTON

OLD HIGHWAY 47

① EASIEST ACCESS FOR THIS SECTION/FISH THE FLAT WATER HERE.

② TOUGH ACCESS-PARK AND HIKE TO RIVER

③ BOAT PUT IN

④ LOTS OF WALKING HERE-BEST TO FLOAT

⑤ GOOD DRY FLY SECTION-LOTS OF SMALLER TROUT

⑥ BOAT TAKE-OUT

15
12
95   HENRY'S FORK
93
21   15
      20
1-84
      15

HENRY'S FORK

NTS

PINE HAVEN TO WARM RIVER/WARM RIVER TO ASHTON

Pine Haven to Warm River

This area is remote and highly rated for scenic beauty and a good spot if you want to get away from humans. However, one must work inordinately hard to get into fish on this water. Over the years I've floated the tricky whitewaters. I've four wheeled into the canyon and descended carefully to fish all the remote sections. I've even dragged a boat down Bear Gulch and floated out. Yet despite these gargantuan efforts, I've not found enough quality fish here to justify all the hard work.

The possible exception is the area upstream of Riverside Campground. Mayfly and caddis hatches on the flat water and a lingering salmon fly hatch make this area quite enjoyable. It's also more easily accessed!

From the Mesa Falls Scenic Byway (old Highway 47) look for any number of woodroads that lead to the canyon. You'll have to park at the canyon rim and hike down to the river. Consult a topographical map and get more information from a local fly shop. If you do venture into the canyon you probably won't find me crowding your space.

Type of Fish
Mostly rainbow trout with increasing numbers of brown trout below Mesa Falls.

Flies To Use
Dry patterns: Stone Fly and standard dry flies.
Nymphs: Wooly Bugger and Sculpin-type streamers.

When to Fish
Most any time, but the best fly fishing is during the Salmon Fly hatch in June.

Seasons & Limits
Seasons and limits can change so consult the Idaho Fish & Game regulation booklet, but generally from Ashton to Riverside campgrounds fish the general season with a 2 fish slot limit.

Rating
Because of the effort involved, a 5.

Warm River to Ashton

This is a very popular section of river to float. Considering the size of this water, big fish don't seem to surface feed here very much. The one exception is during the Salmon Fly hatch in early June. If fishing a dry fly and catching and releasing a boat load of fish from 8" to 12" (with an occasional 16 incher) is what you want, this section is for you.

From Island Park, take the Mesa Falls Scenic Byway (old Highway 47) or Mesa Falls Road to the Warm River. Take the dirt road that crosses the Henry's Fork to the put-in. You can also reach this spot by taking the same highway east, through the town of Ashton.

A note on wading: This section can be waded, but river access is limited. One must walk a lot, either down the bank or along the railroad tracks that parallel the river. Floating is recommended to successfully work this entire section of river. Take-out is either at Ashton (Wendell) Bridge on Highway 191 or at the boat ramp in the backwaters of Ashton Reservoir.

Type of Fish
Mostly rainbow with increasing numbers of browns.

Flies To Use
Dry patterns: Humpy, Elk Hair Caddis, Stimulator, Henryville Caddis, Parachute Adams, Light Cahill, Royal Wulff #12-16.
Nymphs & Terrestrials: Many wet or Soft Hackled patterns, Black Rubber Legs #6-8, Dave's Hopper #8-10.

When to Fish
All season, but this area can be especially good in August and early September when other areas go flat.

Season & Limits
Riverside Campground to Ashton: General season, 2 fish slot limit. Seasons and limits can change, consult the Idaho Fish & Game regulation booklet.

Rating
In early June, a 7. Most other times, a 5.

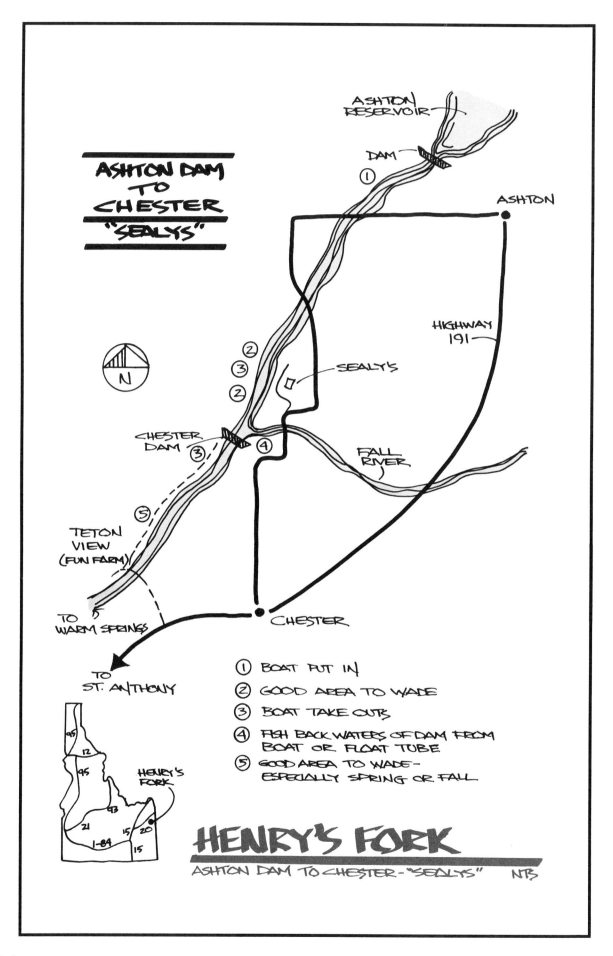

ASHTON DAM TO CHESTER "SEALYS"

ASHTON RESERVOIR

DAM
①

ASHTON

HIGHWAY 191

②
③
②

SEALY'S

N

CHESTER DAM
③
④

FALL RIVER

⑤

TETON VIEW (FUN FARM)

TO WARM SPRINGS

CHESTER

TO ST. ANTHONY

① BOAT PUT IN
② GOOD AREA TO WADE
③ BOAT TAKE OUTS
④ FISH BACK WATERS OF DAM FROM BOAT OR FLOAT TUBE
⑤ GOOD AREA TO WADE - ESPECIALLY SPRING OR FALL

HENRY'S FORK
95
12
95
HENRY'S FORK
43
21
15 20
1-84
15

HENRY'S FORK

ASHTON DAM TO CHESTER - "SEALYS"   NB

Ashton Dam to Chester

This area is commonly referred to as "Sealy's" because of nearby Sealy's farm. Because it's open year around and with its newly established slot limit regulation, fly fishing is better than ever.

Getting to and finding the various fly fishing areas is easy. From Ashton, head west to the Ora Bridge, just below Ashton Dam. Sealy's farm, above Chester dam, is private property but has a public access area. Go to the small town of Chester, just off Highway 20/191. Take Chester Road across Fall River. Just after the road bends right, look for a dirt road on the left with fences and corrals. Look for a farm house in the distance on the right and tall stands of Cottonwood trees bordering the river. Chester dam can be reached from Teton View road. After crossing the river, turn right and follow the road upstream to the dam.

Type of Fish
Mostly rainbow with increasing numbers of brown trout.

Flies To Use

March-April
Hatches can be very heavy, be prepared to fish them all.
Dry patterns: Midges #18-20, Early Blue Winged Olives #18-20, Dirty Olive Caddis #14-16.

May-June
Spring runoff can stop most hatches but also heralds the Salmon Fly.
Dry patterns: Improved Sofa Pillow #4-6, Adams, Adams Parachute #20, Black Midge Pupa, Brassies #18-20, Blue Winged Olives, Light Olive Parachutes, Gray/Olive No-Hackles and Parachute Adams #18-20, Lawson's Henry's Fork Salmon Fly #4-6.
Nymphs: Pheasant Tail, Mason Baetis Nymph #18, Olive Caddis #14-16, Salmon Fly #2-6.

June-July
The real fishing begins. Keep flies reasonably sparse.
Dry patterns: Green/Gray Drake #10, Green Drake Paradun, Pale Morning Dun (P.M.D.), Parachute P.M.D., Gray/Yellow No-Hackles, P.M.D. Thorax #14-20. Also various Caddis #14-18, Red Quill Hen Spinner #10-12 (dry) for the backwaters of Chester Dam.

August
Can be slow.

September 15 - October:
Baetis hatch is spectacular.
Dry patterns: Blue Winged Olive #18-20, Olive Parachute or Thorax flies, Slate Mahogany Dun.

Season & Limits
Chester to Ashton Dam generally open all year with a 2 fish slot limit, none between 8"-16". Seasons and limits can change, consult the Idaho Fish & Game regulation booklet.

When to Fish
Early or late season. From mid to late summer, hatches diminish and weed growth and water levels get high making fishing slow and technical. By late fall, when conditions return to normal the fishing becomes outstanding.

Floating
Because of limited access, floating is the best way to fish this section. If you are unfamiliar with this section of river or boating in general, consult a qualified guide or outfitter. The backwater of Chester Dam must be fished with a boat or float tube. *Chester Dam put-in or take-out:* take Teton View road just North of St. Anthony off Highway 191. Cross the river, turn right, take the mediocre dirt road to the dam. *Ashton Bridge put-in:* at the traffic light in Ashton, turn west to Ashton Dam, cross the river, put-in below the bridge.

Rating
Overall, a 6.

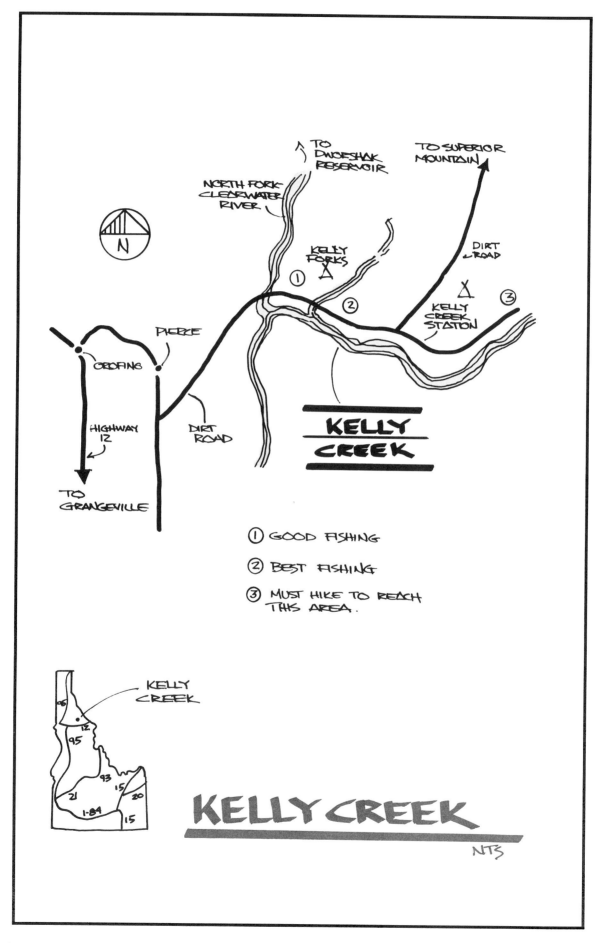

TO DWORSHAK RESERVOIR

TO SUPERIOR MOUNTAIN

NORTH FORK CLEARWATER RIVER

N

KELLY FORKS

DIRT ROAD

① ②

KELLY CREEK STATION

③

PIERCE

OROFINO

KELLY CREEK

HIGHWAY 12

DIRT ROAD

TO GRANGEVILLE

① GOOD FISHING

② BEST FISHING

③ MUST HIKE TO REACH THIS AREA.

KELLY CREEK

95
12
95
93
21   15
1-84   20
15

KELLY CREEK

NTS

Kelly Creek

Kelly Creek is one of the great trout streams in northern Idaho's panhandle region. Special catch and release regulations have helped save the stream's indigenous cutthroat trout, though overall it does lack big fish associated with many blue ribbon streams. A strong population of catchable fish in the 10" to 15" category, with the occasional larger fish, is reason enough to head for Kelley Creek.

Kelley Creek can be reached from the south from Superior, Montana. Most approach from Lewiston or Orofino from the west. Go through the little town of Pierce, Idaho taking state road 11. After some 45 miles (on a good dirt road) look for signs that direct you to the Kelley Creek Ranger Station, where a road parallels the creek.

Type of Fish

Westslope cutthroat.

Equipment to Use

Rods: 4 to 6 weight, 8 1/2' to 9'.
Line: Floating line to match your rod weight. Use split shot to fish nymphs.
Leaders: 4x and 5x, 9' to 12'.
Reel: Mechanical or palm drag.
Wading: Neoprene waders with felt-soled wading shoes or hip boots.

Flies to Use

Dry patterns: Yellow and Olive Stimulator, Royal Wulff, Elk hair Caddis #12-16. Grasshopper patterns #8-10.
Nymphs: Prince, Hare's Ear, regular and beaded #10-16. Flashback, Small Wooly Buggers, #12-16.

When to Fish

Depending on snowpack, runoff delays the good fishing until mid-July. Fall is the best time to fly fish Kelly Creek.

Seasons & Limits

Catch & release, barbless hooks on artificial flies and lures. Check the Idaho Department of Fish and Game regulations booklet.

Accommodations & Services

There is a Forest Service campground with basic facilities at the stream, but that is all.

Rating

A solid 7.5.

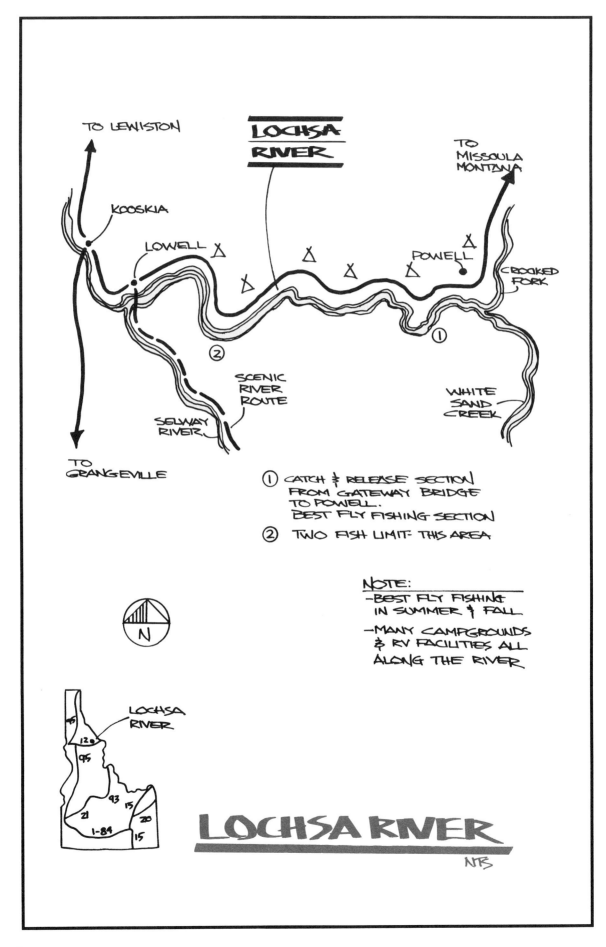

The Lochsa River

*T*he Lochsa is very accessible when you're in the northern part of the state. The Lewis and Clark Highway (Highway 12) parallels this fairly large river most of the way making access fairly routine. The cites of Lowell and Powell are at each end of this portion of the Lochsa. The 30 mile upper river from Gateway Bridge to Powell is catch and release and the best bet for fly fishing success. The 50 mile lower river from Lowell to the Gateway Bridge has good quantities of insects but fewer fish than the upper section.

Limits and catch & release regulations were placed on the Lochsa in an effort to maintain the Westslope cutthroat trout. The results are *lots* of trout between 12" and 14" and many in the 18" category.

Type of Fish
Primarily cutthroat with some rainbow trout.

Known Hatches
Mayflies
September: Little Cream Dun (Centroptilum), Slate Mahogany Dun (Paraleptophlebia).

Stoneflies
April-May: Golden Stone (Archynopteryx).

Equipment to Use
Rods: 5 to 6 weight, 8 1/2' to 9'.
Line: Floating line to match rod weight.
Leaders: 4x to 6x, 9'.
Reels: Mechanical or palm drag.
Wading: Chest-high neoprene waders with felt-soled wading shoes. High water in the spring can make wading difficult.

Flies to Use
Dry patterns: Royal Wulff, Stimulator, Elk Hair Caddis, Adams, Parachute Adams, Light Cahill #12-18, Little Cream Dun #20, Slate Mahogany Dun #10-12, Golden Stone #8, Yellow Stimulator #6-8.
Nymphs: Prince, Hare's Ear, Brown Stone Fly #10-14.

When to Fish
The best fly fishing is in the late summer and fall. In the spring try the lower sections during the whitefish season before runoff occurs.

Season & Limits
General season, usually with a 2 fish limit on the lower river. The upper river is catch and release. Seasons and rules change so refer to the Idaho Fish and Game regulations booklet.

Accommodation & Services
There are various campground and R.V. facilities throughout the region. Hotels, motels, service stations, grocery stores and other services can be found in Lowell and Powell.

Rating
A solid 8 in the fall.

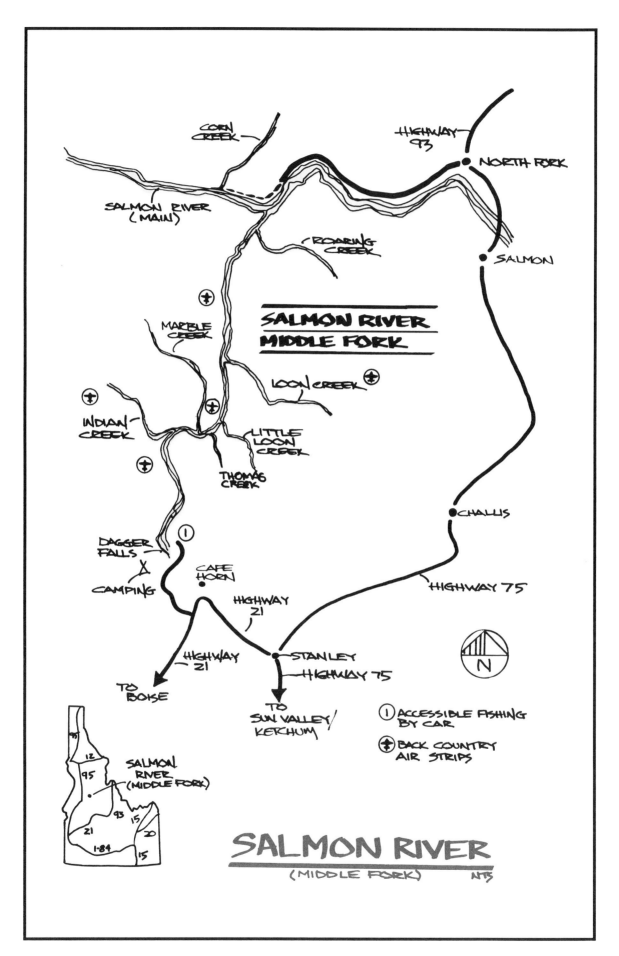

CORN CREEK

HIGHWAY 93

NORTH FORK

SALMON RIVER (MAIN)

ROARING CREEK

SALMON

SALMON RIVER MIDDLE FORK

MARBLE CREEK

LOON CREEK

INDIAN CREEK

LITTLE LOON CREEK

THOMAS CREEK

CHALLIS

DAGGER FALLS

CAMPING

CAPE HORN

HIGHWAY 21

HIGHWAY 75

N

HIGHWAY 21

STANLEY

HIGHWAY 75

TO BOISE

TO SUN VALLEY / KETCHUM

① ACCESSIBLE FISHING BY CAR

✚ BACK COUNTRY AIR STRIPS

95
12
95
SALMON RIVER (MIDDLE FORK)
93 15
21
1-84
20
15

SALMON RIVER

(MIDDLE FORK)   NTS

The Salmon River
Middle Fork

*T*hrough this pristine, scenic wilderness flow crystal clear waters that now contain an abundance of Westslope cutthroat trout. Over-fishing nearly depleted the cutthroats, but catch & release regulations placed in effect in 1970 have restored the fish to near overpopulation. Now the most novice fly fisher will catch fish from this beautiful river.

A portion of the river can be reached from Highway 21 from Stanley by taking the gravel road to Dagger Falls. The remaining 100 miles can only be accessed by boat, or by small planes that use various mountain airstrips. If you plan to fly in, contact an experienced backcountry pilot.

Lack of access and crowds is one reason the Middle Fork is one of the most popular 3-6 day whitewater float trips in Idaho. You'll need a Forest Service permit (Salmon, ID) to do this, or take a trip with an outfitter. This is good idea. With class 2-4 rapids the Middle Fork is not for the inexperienced.

Type of Fish

Primarily cutthroat trout, some steelhead and steelhead smolts and a few rainbow.

Equipment to Use

Rods: 5-6 weight, 8' to 9 1/2'.
Line: Floating line to match rod weight.
Leaders: 4x to 5x, 9'.
Reels: Palm or mechanical drag.
Wading: Chest-high neoprene waders with felt-soled wading shoes.

Flies to Use

When people ask what flies to use here, I jokingly say "Yes". More precisely, take the following: Royal Wulff #14, Yellow Humpy #14, Elk Hair Caddis #10-14, Golden Stone #10, Dave's Hopper #8.

When to Fish

Early season runoff can affect conditions, but generally, starting July 4th the river fishes well. From August 1st to season's end is prime.

Seasons & Limits

Restricted season and catch & release except near Daggar falls area. Consult the Idaho Fish and game regulations booklet.

Accommodations & Services

Riverside camping only. This is remote fly fishing, bring whatever you need and pack it out.

Rating

Only because it lacks large fish, an 8.5.

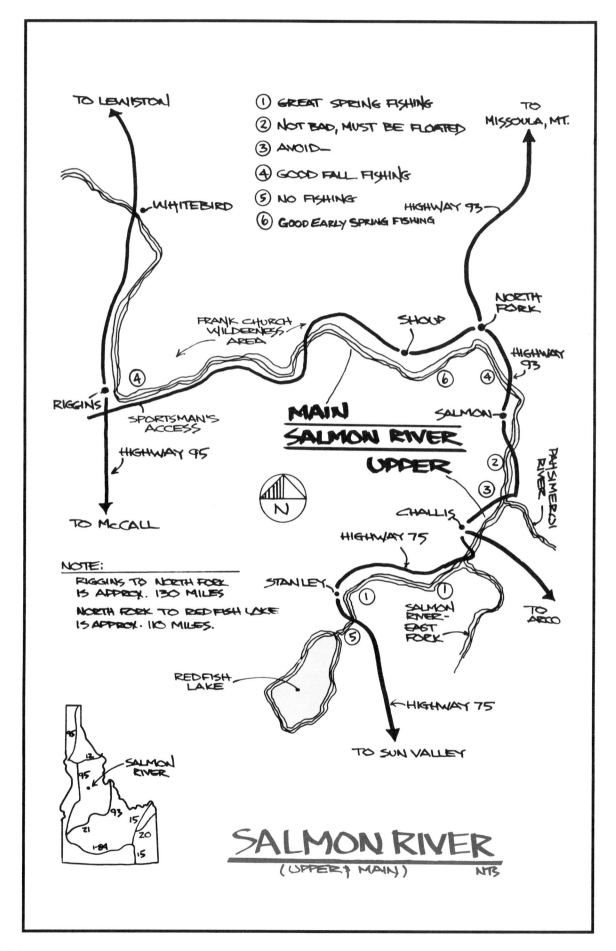

TO LEWISTON

① GREAT SPRING FISHING
② NOT BAD, MUST BE FLOATED
③ AVOID
④ GOOD FALL FISHING
⑤ NO FISHING
⑥ GOOD EARLY SPRING FISHING

TO MISSOULA, MT.

WHITEBIRD

HIGHWAY 93

FRANK CHURCH WILDERNESS AREA

NORTH FORK

SHOUP

HIGHWAY 93

④

⑥ ④

RIGGINS

MAIN
SALMON RIVER
UPPER

SALMON

SPORTSMAN'S ACCESS

HIGHWAY 95

②

PAHSIMEROI RIVER

③

N

CHALLIS

TO McCALL

HIGHWAY 75

TO ARCO

NOTE:
RIGGINS TO NORTH FORK IS APPROX. 130 MILES
NORTH FORK TO REDFISH LAKE IS APPROX. 110 MILES.

STANLEY

①

①

SALMON RIVER- EAST FORK

⑤

REDFISH LAKE

← HIGHWAY 75

TO SUN VALLEY

95

12

75

SALMON RIVER

93

21

15

20

I-84

15

SALMON RIVER
(UPPER & MAIN)

NTB

Salmon River
Upper & Main Sections

*F*rom its origins in the Sawtooth range, the upper Salmon flows north through the mountains to the small village of North Fork, a distance of about 170 miles. The river then heads west on a 450 mile journey of whitewater and runs going through the rugged canyons and mountains of the 2.25 million acre "Frank Church River of No Return" Wilderness area. This middle section is best fished with a boat. The Salmon eventually meets the Snake River at Hell's Canyon on the Idaho-Oregon border. For us fly fishers, lets consider the upper and main sections.

The upper section is paralleled by Highway 75 which affords good river access. Part of the middle section, from North Fork to Corn Creek has varying degrees of road and river access. From Corn Creek down-river it's pretty much "boat only".

To get to the upper section of the Salmon one can take Highway 75 from Sun Valley/Ketchum and Stanley. From eastern Idaho take any Highway to Arco and then get on Highway 93 north to Challis.

Mountain scenery and wilderness aside, the steelhead runs now get most of the attention when considering this river. Hatchery and natives return from the sea in September, some running up to 20 pounds. If you are new to this river or to steelheading, a competent local guide would be a worth-while investment.

A selection of trout and dolly varden (bull trout) up to 20" offer some fly fishing challenges though they receive less notoriety than their sea-running cousins. There is more than enough fish in this river to please the fly angler.

Type of Fish

There are steelhead available during their spawning runs. Whitefish, rainbow, some bull trout, cutthroat and steelhead smolt can make fly fishing here rewarding for everyone.

Equipment to Use

Trout
Rods: 4 to 7 weight rods, 8-1/2' to 9-1/2'.
Line: Floating and sink-tip lines to match the weight of your rod.
Leaders: 4x or 5x, 9'.
Reel: Palm drag is fine.

Steelhead
Rods: 6 to 9 weight, 9' to 9-1/2'.
Line: Both floating and sink tip-lines to match the weight of your rod.
Leaders: 0x or 1x, 7' to 9'.
Reel: Mechanical drag.
Wading: Chest-high neoprenes with felt-soled wading shoes, stream cleats and a wading staff. Consider floating below Challis.

Flies to Use

Trout
General patterns such as Royal Wulff, Humpy, Elk Hair Caddis, Caddis pupa in sizes #12-14 and Dave's Hopper #8-10.

Steelhead
Fall: Green Butted Skunk, Skykomish Sunrise, Silver Hil-
ton, Thor's & Egg Sucking Black Leech, Purple Peril, Marabou Wing, Hair Wing #4-8.
Spring: Add to the above a small egg pattern in cream, burned orange or light pink #8-10.

When to Fish

About April 1st fly fishing between the East Fork of the Salmon and Redfish Lake starts getting good. In the fall, most of the fish are between the Riggins/Whitebird area upstream to the city of Salmon. Jet boats and wide, deep river make the Whitebird area and the section between the cities of North Fork and the city of Salmon the best places to fly fish. *Note:* a major hatchery and collection point for returning fish is located on the Pahsimeroi River at the confluence at Ellis. This area can be a real circus.

Seasons & Limits

The season and limits can vary for trout and steelhead, so consult the Idaho Department of Fish and Game regulations booklet. The steelhead season is usually September 15 to November 31 and March 20 to April 30. In Spring be careful to avoid walking through spawning areas and beds.

Accommodation and Services

Supplies and very adequate accommodations are available in Salmon, Challis, Stanley and Riggins. Campgrounds, when the snow is gone, are available up and down the river.

Rating

For spring steelhead a solid 8. For trout a 2.5.

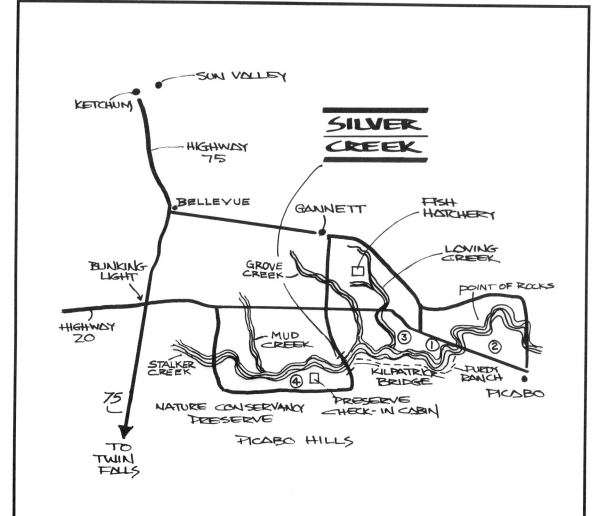

SILVER
CREEK

SUN VALLEY
KETCHUM
HIGHWAY 75
BELLEVUE
GANNETT
FISH HATCHERY
LOVING CREEK
BLINKING LIGHT
GROVE CREEK
POINT OF ROCKS
HIGHWAY 20
MUD CREEK
③
①
②
STALKER CREEK
KILPATRICK BRIDGE
PURDY RANCH
④
PICABO
75
NATURE CONSERVANCY PRESERVE
PRESERVE CHECK-IN CABIN
PICABO HILLS
TO TWIN FALLS

NOTE:
SILVER CREEK
IS 35 MILES
FROM
SUN VALLEY

① MUST FLOAT TUBE—
PRIVATE PROPERTY

② BIG TROUT HERE &
GREAT BROWN DRAKE HATCH

③ PRIVATE ACCESS,
FLOAT TUBE NEEDED
CATCH & RELEASE

④ LOTS OF FLY FISHERS
IN THIS AREA—
CATCH & RELEASE

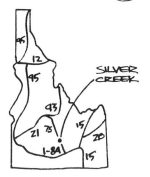

SILVER CREEK

SILVER CREEK

NTB

Silver Creek

*I*nternationally famous "The Creek" as locals refer to it, is perhaps the finest piece of dry fly water one can find. It's also one of the largest, pure spring-fed stream in this country. Silver Creek's abundant food supply supports numerous and large trout, to which one's fly presentation must be near perfect. Moreover, fly imitations must be precise in size, color and profile. Sound challenging? It is.

The upper section of Silver Creek is delineated by the Nature Conservancy Preserve where trout and fly fishers are abundant. The Purdy Ranch section, downstream from the preserve, is private access only. Here the trout population is very strong, but a float tube is required to reach them. The Point of Rocks area has very big trout, though fewer in numbers than in the other sections. This is the Brown Drake hatch area. The basic information needed to fly fish all sections of Silver Creek is summarized on this page.

From Sun Valley/Ketchum take Highway 75, 35 miles south to Gannet where signs direct you to the Nature Conservancy Preserve. Other sections of river are reached off of Highway 20. From Highway 75, turn east at the flashing signal light at the intersection of Highway 20.

Type of Fish
Rainbow, brown and some brook trout.

Known Hatches
These extensive hatches are presented on page 51.

Equipment to Use
Rods: 3 to 5 weight, 8 1/2' to 9'.
Lines: Floating.
Leaders: 5x to 7x with 8x for small mayflies.
Reels: Mechanical or palm drag.
Wading: Chest-high neoprene waders, felt-soled wading boots.

Flies to Use

June 1-10: Brown Drake hatch in Point of Rocks area, with Duns and Spinners fished at dusk.
Dry patterns: Brown Drake #10, Brown Drake Paradrake, Partridge Spinner #10, Pale Morning Dun #16-18.
Nymphs: Brown Drake #10.

June-August 15: Pale Morning Duns peak first week of August. Duns emerge July-Aug. at dusk. See June 1-10 flies above, plus these:
Dry patterns: Gray/Yellow No-Hackle, Parachute Pale Morning Dun, Yellow Hen Spinner #16-18.

June-September: Late morning hatch of Light Olive Quill Spinner. Mayfly hatch continuous. Peak hatch of Speckle Dun and Spinner 8/25 - 9/20. See June-Aug. 15 flies above, plus these:
Dry patterns: Little Olive Quill Spinner #22, Mason Loop Wing Spinner #22, Red Quill Hen Spinner, Light Olive Parachute, Gray/Yellow No-Hackle #22, Gray Partridge Parachute, Slate/Gray No-Hackle, Partridge Hen Spinner #18-20.
Nymphs: Red Quill Emerger tied sparsely, Callibaetis #14 -18.

July 20-August: Big morning Trico Spinner falls. See June-Sept. flies above, plus these:
Dry patterns: Trico or White Winged Black #22, White/Black Cul-De-Canard (C.D.C.) Spinner #22, White/Black Hen Spinner #22, Mason Loop Wing Trico #22, White/Black No-Hackle #22.

August 15-September 10: Late morning/early afternoon Small Pale Morning Dun hatch. See July 20-Aug. flies above, plus these:
Dry patterns: Small Pale Morning Dun, Pale Morning Dun Parachute, Grey/Yellow No-Hackle #20.

August 25-September 1: Sporadic afternoon Baetis hatch. See Aug. 15-Sept. 10 flies above, plus these:
Dry patterns: Little Bright Olive Dun, Little Olive Parachute #22, Speckle Dun & Spinner #16-20.

September 20-October: Afternoon Blue Winged Olive hatch.
Dry patterns: Blue Winged Olive #20, Little Olive Parachute and Gray/Olive No-Hackle #20.
Nymphs: Mason Baetis Nymph #18, Pheasant Tail #18.

October: Inconsistent but good Slate Mahogany Dun or Paralep hatch. See Sept. 20-Oct. flies above, plus these:
Dry patterns: Slate Mahogany Dun, Paralep #16, Brown Parachute, Slate/Mahogany No-Hackle #16.

When to Fish
You can fish summer to winter, but the best fishing is mid-summer into late fall. June hatches can be inconsistent but improve with the passing months.

Seasons & Limits
Consult the Idaho Department of Fish and Game regulations booklet. The Nature Conservancy and Purdy Ranch areas are catch and release, barbless flies. Below Highway 20, 2 fish limit, none between 12"-16".

Accommodations & Services
Some camping is available at the Fish & Game hatchery and the Point of Rocks Sportsman's Access area. Plenty of lodging and services can be found 25-35 miles north on Highway 75 in the towns of Hailey, Ketchum and Sun Valley or 60 miles south on Highway 75 in Twin Falls.

Rating
For classic dry fly fishing in a challenging situation, Silver Creek is a solid 10.

❖ 33 ❖

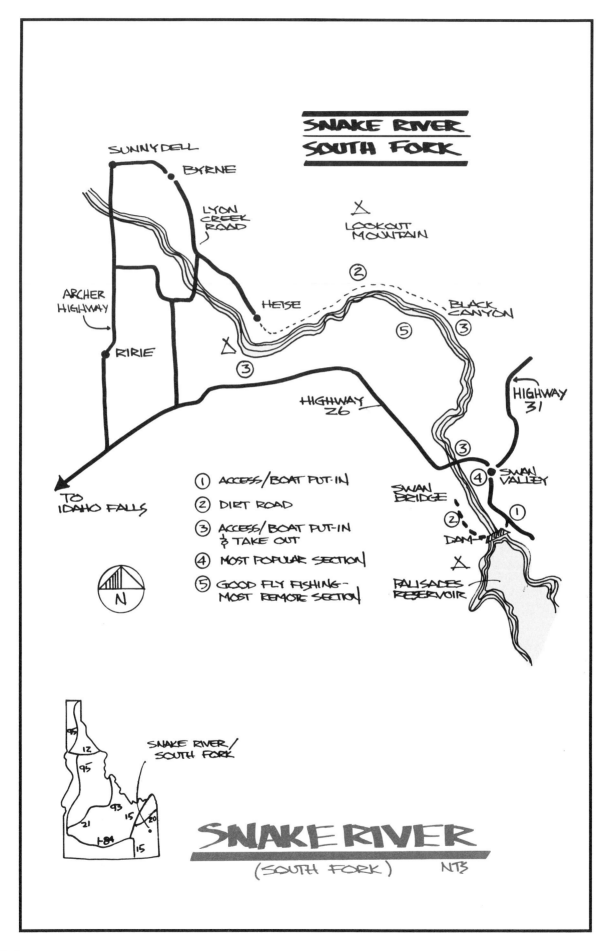

SNAKE RIVER
SOUTH FORK

SUNNYDELL
BYRNE
LYON CREEK ROAD
ARCHER HIGHWAY
RIRIE
HEISE
LOOKOUT MOUNTAIN
②
⑤
③ BLACK CANYON
③
HIGHWAY 26
HIGHWAY 31
③
④ SWAN VALLEY
SWAN BRIDGE
②
①
DAM
PALISADES RESERVOIR
TO IDAHO FALLS

① ACCESS/BOAT PUT-IN
② DIRT ROAD
③ ACCESS/BOAT PUT-IN & TAKE OUT
④ MOST POPULAR SECTION
⑤ GOOD FLY FISHING – MOST REMOTE SECTION

N

SNAKE RIVER/ SOUTH FORK

95
12
95
93
15
20
21
I-84
15

SNAKE RIVER
(SOUTH FORK)   NTS

The Snake River South Fork

*T*he 60 miles of the South Fork of the Snake River is one of the great river systems in the state of Idaho. Starting in Wyoming, the South Fork's fertile and rowdy waters produce huge fish. Fly fishers can cast to some of the largest cutthroat and brown trout in Idaho. The state record brown (some 35 pounds) was taken from these waters.

Most of the great fly fishing is in two sections: From Palisades Dam, 10 miles downstream to Swan Valley bridge and from the Swan Valley bridge to Black Canyon or Table Rock. The upper section (dam to Swan Valley bridge) has easier access and is a shorter float and hence, is the most popular section. The lower section is just as good but more remote. This river is very popular, and one had better be prepared to share the water with other people and boats during the peak season.

The South Fork is big water, and while it can be waded in most spots, the most practical way to fish the river is by boat. There is a Salmon Fly hatch around mid-July that moves 4-5 miles upstream each day which can send trout into a feeding frenzy. This can be some fantastic fly fishing. Salmon Fly or not, a day fly fishing on the South Fork will be a day long remembered.

The easiest way to the South Fork of the Snake is to take Highway 26 from Idaho Falls toward Jackson Hole, Wyoming. Cross the South Fork at the Swan Valley bridge and then drive along the river upstream to Palisades Dam. Take-outs in the lower section can be accessed through the small community of Sunnydell traveling upstream to Table Rock and Black Canyon.

Type of Fish

Cutthroat, German brown, some rainbow, a few mackinaw that sneak in from the reservoir and mountain whitefish.

Equipment to Use

Rods: 6 to 8 weight, 9'.
Line: Floating or sink tip to match rod weight.
Leaders: 1x to 5x, 7' - 9'.
Reel: Mechanical or palm drag.
Wading: Chest-high neoprene waders with felt-soled wading shoes. The South Fork of the Snake has some treacherous sections, so be very careful when wading.

Flies to Use

Dry patterns: Parachute Adams, Light Cahill #8-18. Elk Hair and Henryville Caddis #12-16. Soft Hackled flies for the emerging pupa and Grasshoppers #12-16.
Wet patterns: Super Renegade, Black, Black & Olive, Brown Variegated Wooly Buggers #2-6, Jansen Little Rainbow Trout #8.
July Salmon Fly hatch: Henry's Fork Stone, Bird's Stonefly #4-8, Black Rubber Legs Nymph #4-6.

When to Fish

The mid-July Salmon Fly hatch is great but limited in duration. High water can be a problem in the summer. With more consistent water levels, September and October has great fish and may be the best fall fly fishing in the state.

Season & Limits

Most years one can fish the entire river year-around. From the mouth upstream to the cable at Heise, 2 trout limit, none between 8"-16". Check the Idaho Department of Fish and Game regulations booklet for more information.

Accommodations & Services

Camping, car parks, boat launches and other facilities are spread along most of the river. Motels and lodges are available in Idaho Falls and Swan Valley. Luxury accommodations are available at Palisade Resort Lodge.

Rating

In the late summer and especially fall, this river rates as a solid 10. Mid-summer, with the exception of the Salmon Fly hatch, high and inconsistent water levels can drop this to a 6.5.

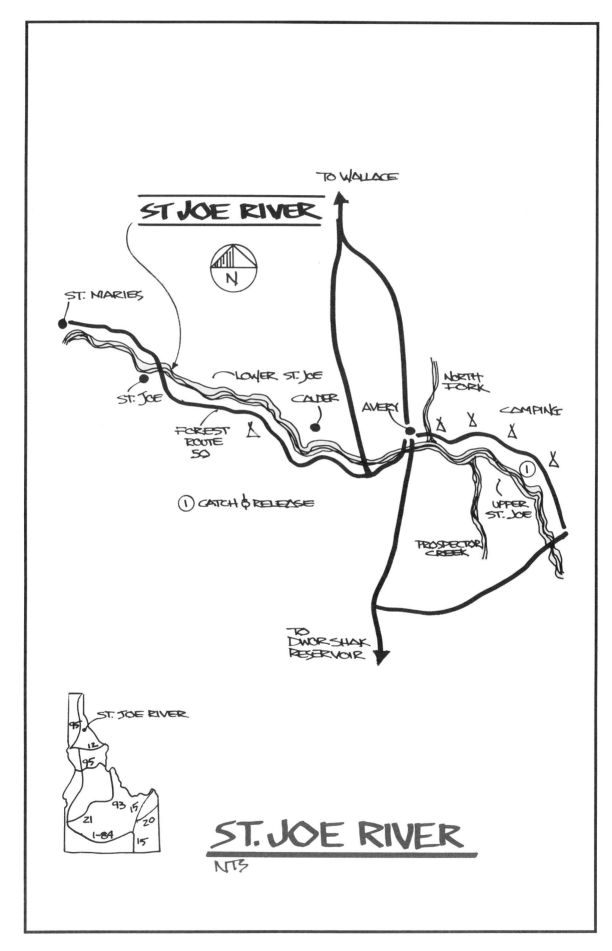

ST. JOE RIVER

NTS

The St. Joe River

*T*he section from the town of Avery to the headwaters are designated a Wild and Scenic River. The eastern stretch of river is a Wild Trout Trophy fishery. The lower sections feature fine bass fishing. No wonder residents of northern Idaho consider the St. Joe one of the best rivers to fish in the entire state.

The lower river, between St. Marie's and Prospector Creek is big water, making wading fairly difficult. The smaller upper section can be waded except for the many deep pools. In addition, one must often maneuver around or cast from house-sized boulders. This is not a fly fishing river for youngsters or for people with problems getting around. This aside, the river and surrounding area is beautiful and if you are in the northern part of Idaho in mid-summer or fall the St. Joe should be visited.

From southern Idaho, go to St. Marie's (south of Lake Coeur d'Alene) and take Highway 5 up the river. From the north take Highway 10 to Wallace, Idaho. In town turn south on the road leading to Avery. At Avery, you can drive up and down river.

Type of Fish

Primarily cutthroat, with some dolly varden and bass in the lower sections.

Equipment to Use

Rods: 5 to 6 weight, 8 1/2' to 9'.
Line: Floating and sink-tip lines to match rod weight.
Leaders: 3x to 5x, 7 1/2' to 9'.
Reels: Palm or mechanical drag.
Wading: Chest-high neoprene waders with felt-soled wading shoes.

Flies to Use

Dry patterns: Royal Wulff, Humpy, Stimulator, Elk Hair Caddis #12-16.
Nymphs: Prince Nymph and Hares Ear #10-14, Black, Brown and Black/Olive Flashabou Wooly Bugger #8-12.

When to Fish

Because of runoff, good fishing does not begin until mid-July. As water levels drop fishing gets better.

Seasons & Limits

Generally from the town of St. Marie's upstream to Prospector Creek there is a 1 fish limit (must be over 14"). Above Prospector Creek it's all catch and release, barbless artificial flies and lures. This season usually runs from Memorial weekend to September 10. Seasons and limits can change, consult the Idaho Department of Fish and Game regulations booklet.

Accommodations & Services

Campgrounds are located up and down the river, but as you move upstream they tend to get smaller. Services, food, gas etc. are available at Avery and St. Marie's.

Rating

A 6.5.

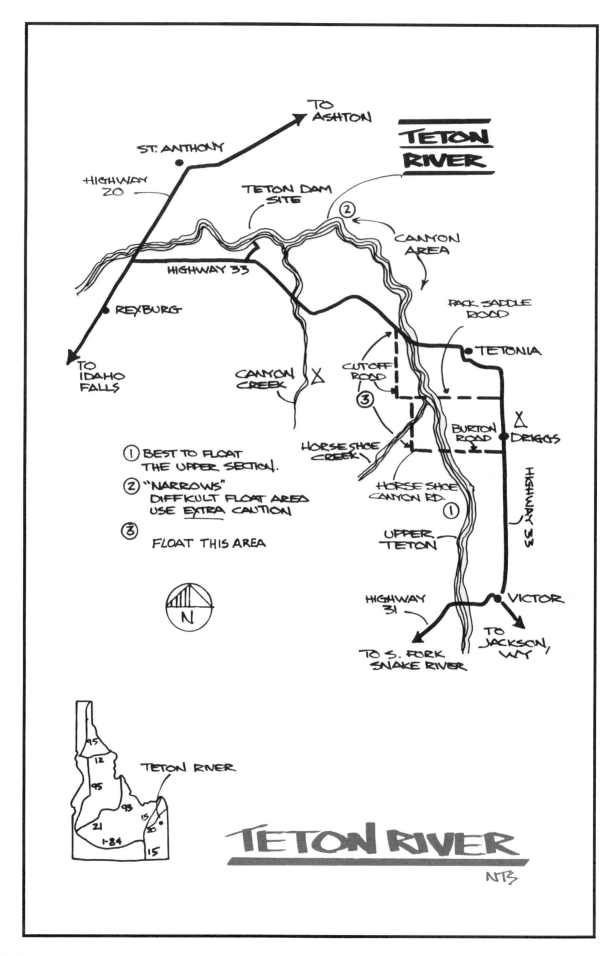

TETON RIVER

TO ASHTON

ST. ANTHONY

HIGHWAY 20

TETON DAM SITE

② CANYON AREA

HIGHWAY 33

REXBURG

PACK SADDLE ROAD

TETONIA

TO IDAHO FALLS

CANYON CREEK

CUT OFF ROAD

③

HORSESHOE CREEK

BURTON ROAD

DRIGGS

① BEST TO FLOAT THE UPPER SECTION.

② "NARROWS" DIFFICULT FLOAT AREA USE EXTRA CAUTION

③ FLOAT THIS AREA

HORSE SHOE CANYON RD.

①

UPPER TETON

HIGHWAY 33

N

HIGHWAY 31

VICTOR

TO S. FORK SNAKE RIVER

TO JACKSON, WY.

95
12
95
93
21
1-84
15
15

TETON RIVER

TETON RIVER

NTS

The Teton River

*I*f you are in the eastern part of Idaho or northwestern Wyoming and looking for a smooth meadow-type stream with good insect activity and rising trout, try the Teton. Or, if you're looking for an exciting, fast flowing canyon-type river, the Teton is also a good bet. A bit of historical background is important however, if one is to evaluate this river.

The Teton was once one of eastern Idaho's greatest fly fishing streams. A series of problems including poor farming and ranching practices, siltation, and the failure of the Teton Dam in 1976 changed the river drastically. Since the dam failure and resulting flood, reclamation funds have helped restore the upper meadow section and the canyon above the original dam site. This canyon or "The Narrows" still has some very good fishing above the backwaters of the dam (Bitch Creek). It's a treacherous float however. As Rene Harrop, the famous fly tier from St. Anthony says, "It still claims more McKenzie River drift boats per mile than any other river I know." Below the dam can be just as tricky. By all accounts the upper Teton should continue to improve and hopefully surpass its former glory.

The easiest way to The Teton River is to take Highway 33 east from Rexburg (or west from Jackson Wyoming) to Driggs, Idaho. Look for the Sportsman's Access signs on Highway 33.

Type of Fish

Primarily cutthroat and rainbow.

Equipment to Use

Rods: 3 to 6 weight, with 6 wt. preferred on the lower river, 8' to 9 1/2'.
Lines: Match floating line to rod weight.
Leaders: 5x to 7x, 9' to 12'.
Reels: Mechanical or palm drag.
Wading: Chest-high neoprene waders and felt-soled wading boots. Wading is possible, but for the best fly fishing (given high silt accumulations) most of the upper Teton should be floated.

Flies to Use

Canyon Section
Dry patterns: Henry's Fork Golden Stone (June), Yellow and Olive Stimulator #8-10, Elk Hair Caddis #12-16, Dave's Regular and Parachute Hopper and other standard dries.
Nymphs: Golden Stone.

Meadow Section
Dry patterns: Pale Morning Dun #16-20, Parachute Pale Morning Dun, Thorax Pale Morning Dun, Gray/Yellow No-Hackle, Harrop Hair Wing Dun, Little Olive Parachute in appropriate sizes, Blue Winged Olive #18-22. Black, Brown Ant #8-14, Black Crowe Beetle #14-18, Yellow and Green Dave's Hopper, Henry's Fork Hopper # 8-12.
Nymphs: Mason Baetis, Pheasant Tail #18, Various Caddis #16-20, Tan, Black, Olive Partridge Caddis #14 -20.

When to Fish

Mid-July to the end of August are the best fly fishing periods.

Season & Limits

The general season is Memorial Day Weekend through November 30. Other limits apply and regulations can change, so consult the Idaho Fish and Game regulations booklet.

Accommodations and Services

Lodging, camping, food, gas, and groceries are available in Driggs.

Rating

Because of stream degradation a 4.5 to 5. If reclamation succeeds, a 7.5.

Comments On
Other Rivers, Streams & Creeks

Idaho has many more rivers, streams and creeks that can provide gratifying fly fishing than those highlighted in this guide. These "other" waters, for reasons including drought, declining water quality, lack of large trout, access problems and other issues, are not afforded detailed attention in this guide. They deserve mention however. And who knows, one just might be the kind of place you've been looking for.

Falls River

Located in eastern Idaho between the towns of Ashton and St. Anthony, Falls River meets the Henry's Fork just above the Chester dam. Although not well known, it is one of the more productive rivers in this part of the state, especially the upper end. It has it all; quality trout, great hatches and a wonderful Salmon Fly hatch in mid-June. Floating is the best way to access and fly fish the entire river. Guided float trips are not permitted.

Wading can be difficult. In fact, wading Falls River makes the Madison, Box Canyon on the Henry's Fork, and the South Fork of the Boise seem easy. The stream bed is very slick and felt-soled wading shoes and or stream cleats are needed. Access to the lower river is not particularly easy either. But if you are a capable wader and can overcome some inconvenience, the upper reaches of Fall River can be a real good fly fishing outing. It's wise to check at area fly shops about access points before venturing forth.

Little Wood River

Located south of Silver Creek, its main source of water, the Little Wood River has beautiful pools, runs and riffles leading one to believe this is a trout haven. Because it flows through hot desert, this fine river is best fished in the fall and late spring.

The Little Wood received plantings of brown trout in the early 1970's (the source of the browns in Silver Creek today) that accompany the stream's rainbow trout population. In the fall, Baetis or Blue Winged Olives appear in the afternoon transforming a no-fish day into one that can yield surprisingly large trout. Flies to use: Hopper, Wooly Bugger and in the fall, Parachute Adams #16-18.

Selway River

Located high in the Selway/Bitterroot Wilderness Area, the Selway's trout population can be staggering, with 18" cutthroat commonplace. The river, which enters the Lochsa River at Lowell, is also one of the most pristine fly fishing environments in Idaho.

The lower section is accessible from the confluence upstream to Selway Falls and all types of fishing methods with general fish limits are permitted. As a result, the lower section tends to be less productive. The best way to access and fly fish the more productive upper river, is by floating. But floating is limited by a permit system (for the public and outfitters) and such a trip must be planned far in advance.

The river and put-in site can be reached from the long and winding Magruder Corridor Road out of Darby, Montana. The easiest and quickest way in is to fly into Moose Creek a 6,000' Forest Service airstrip used for fire fighting. Unfortunately, you are still limited to only a few parts of the river. Also, watch for rattlesnakes along the banks when going into or getting out of the water. For these reasons and because of the limited floating opportunities, I've placed the Selway in this section of this guide. With criticism likely to come my way, I'll probably regret this decision. But everything aside, if you get a chance to float the Selway, take it. You won't be disappointed. Flies to use: Royal Wulff #14 , Yellow Humpy #14, Elk Hair Caddis #14, Golden Stone #10, Dave's Hopper #8.

Warm River/Robinson Creek

If your idea of bliss is casting a dry fly in a stream loaded with 8" to 10" trout, the Warm River and Robinson Creek is your kind of place. Both enter the Henry's Fork at Warm River east of Ashton, thus the name, "The Three River Area."

The lower section of Warm River can be accessed from its confluence or by descending down the bank from old Highway 47. Ask for some directions from local fly shops if you plan to fish the upper end. Robinson Creek can also be accessed from Warm River or from the road, upstream, that parallels and crosses the creek. Both rivers have good quantities of small fish. Horseshoe Lake, located east of these rivers can also be quite fun, but you will need a boat or float tube. Use standard attractor patterns #14-18 on all these waters.

SECTION II
Selected
Lakes & Reservoirs

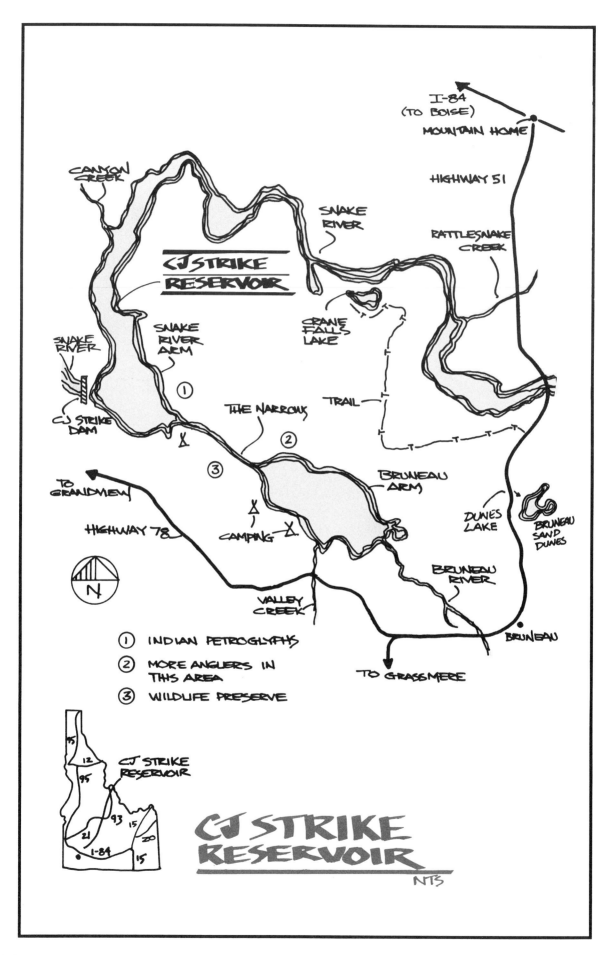

CANYON
CREEK

SNAKE
RIVER

I-84
(TO BOISE)

MOUNTAIN HOME

HIGHWAY 51

RATTLESNAKE
CREEK

CJ STRIKE
RESERVOIR

SNAKE
RIVER
ARM

CRANE
FALLS
LAKE

SNAKE
RIVER

CJ STRIKE
DAM

①

THE NARROWS

TRAIL

②

③

BRUNEAU
ARM

TO
GRANDVIEW

HIGHWAY 78

CAMPING

DUNES
LAKE

BRUNEAU
SAND
DUNES

N

BRUNEAU
RIVER

VALLEY
CREEK

BRUNEAU

① INDIAN PETROGLYPHS

② MORE ANGLERS IN
THIS AREA

③ WILDLIFE PRESERVE

TO GRASSMERE

95

12

95

CJ STRIKE
RESERVOIR

93

15

21

20

I-84

15

CJ STRIKE
RESERVOIR
NTS

C.J. Strike Reservoir

*I*daho has a great alternative to, or respite from, fly fishing for trout: warm water fish in ponds, pothole desert lakes and even the lower sections of major rivers like the St. Joe and Snake. Plus, fly fishing for bluegill, crappie and bass is generally best when the trout season is either closed or when most waters are unfishable. C.J. Strike Reservoir and the Bruneau area, the so called "Desert Fishing Oasis" are two of the best places for pan fish and bass in the state.

Located 20 miles south of Mountain Home, (from Interstate 84 take Highway 51 south towards Bruneau) C.J. Strike is comprised of two reservoirs, the Snake River arm and the Bruneau arm. There are more and larger bass in the Snake River section, but the insistent spring winds can be bothersome. The Bruneau arm, which consists of "The Narrows" and the upper deep section has a good supply of fish but tends to have more anglers. Nearby Crane Falls Lake also provides excellent fishing.

Type of Fish

Abundant populations of bass, bluegill, crappie and perch. There are also trout, though they're tougher to find when the waters warm.

Equipment to Use

Bluegill, crappie perch
Rods: 3 and 4 weight, 8' to 9'.
Lines: Floating and sometimes sink tip.
Leaders: 4x and 5x, 9' to 12'.
Reel: Palm drag.
Wading: Bank fishing or wading is ok with chest-high waders and felt-soled wading boots. It's best to fish from a boat or float tube.

Bass
Rods: 6 and 7 weight, 8' to 9 1/2'.
Lines: Floating and sometimes sink tip.
Leaders: 4x and 5x, 9' to 12'.
Reel: Mechanical drag or single action type.
Wading: Bank fishing or wading is ok with chest-high waders and felt-soled wading boots. It's best to fish from a boat or float tube.

Flies to Use

Bluegill, crappie perch
Subsurface: Brown Ostrich, Marabou Nymph, small leeches, small lead-head jigs, small Griddle Bug in black, brown, bright olive, chartreuse and yellow, #8-#10.
Surface: Foam Spider, Cricket, small popping bugs in black, green, yellow and white #10-12, (#8-10 for crappie).

Bass
Subsurface: Wooly Bugger with flashabou, beaded eyes or regular, in a variety of colors. Streamer patterns imitating chubs, yellow, black perch imitation tied Matuka style.
Surface: Poppers in many colors.

When to Fish

Overall, May through mid-June can be the most productive as spawning activity is at its peak. Water temperatures should be in the low 60°'s for good success. Fish shallow areas along banks and outcropping structure, flooded willows, weeds and grasses as well as small incoming streams. Also look for white-ish areas near the shoreline indicating spawning beds. September through November bass are loading up before winter and will strike readily and trout are up closer to the surface.
Tips: For subsurface fishing use a steady retrieve at various speeds. Cast poppers at target then "pop" the bug by sharply snapping the rod back once. While the poppers is resting on the surface wiggle rod back and forth to make it quiver.

Season & Limits

C.J. Strike can be fished year-around. Consult the Idaho Department of Fish and Game regulations booklet for any changes or limits.

Accommodations & Services

You can stay in Mountain Home, but it's easier to camp at the campgrounds at either reservoir. Black Sands Resort on the south shore of the Snake arm also has lodging. Near the dam on the north shore are displays of prehistoric Indian petroglyphs. An interesting side trip is nearby Bruneau Sand Dunes State Park and Bruneau Lake. This water, now pumped from the Snake River, probably has more bluegill and bass than C.J. Strike reservoir!

Rating

When conditions and water temperature are right, a 7.

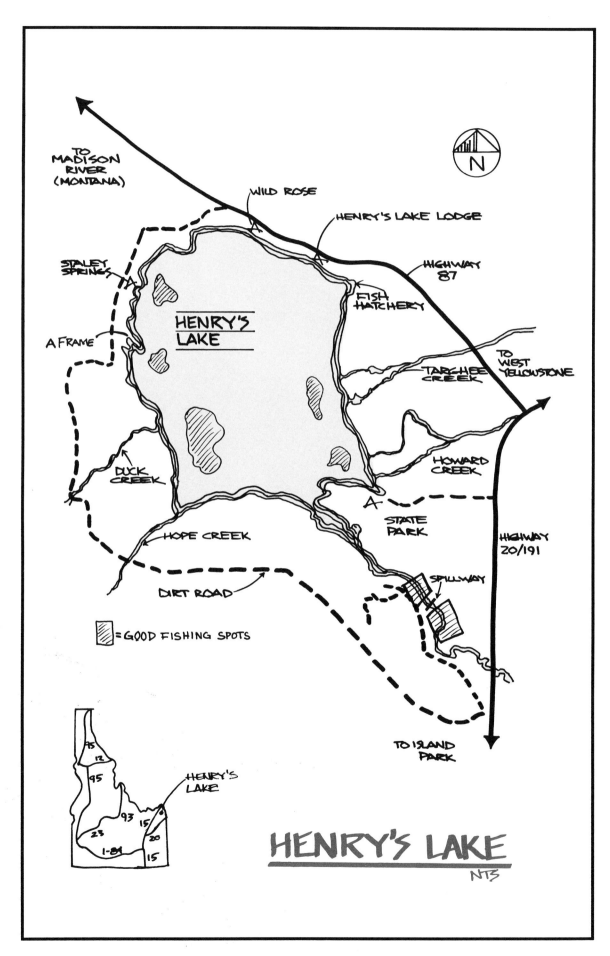

TO
MADISON
RIVER
(MONTANA)

N

WILD ROSE

HENRY'S LAKE LODGE

HIGHWAY 87

STALEY
SPRINGS

FISH
HATCHERY

A FRAME

HENRY'S
LAKE

TO
WEST
YELLOWSTONE

TARGHEE
CREEK

DUCK
CREEK

HOWARD
CREEK

HOPE CREEK

STATE
PARK

HIGHWAY
20/191

DIRT ROAD

SPILLWAY

= GOOD FISHING SPOTS

TO ISLAND
PARK

95
12
95
93 15
23 20
1-84 15

HENRY'S
LAKE

HENRY'S LAKE

NTS

Henry's Lake

*H*enry's Lake is probably the finest fly fishing lake in Idaho. If you know of a better one, you might want to keep it to yourself. The 4.5 by 3.5 mile lake is shallow with an average depth of 18 feet. Much of the water comes from springs and the lake's rich aquatic growth provides tremendous nourishment for fish.

The majority of fishing done on "Hank's Pond" is from a boat or float tube. Fly fishing from the bank or by wading is limited. And despite what appears to be rising fish, Henry's does not fish with dry flies. Leave floating lines in your car.

The lake consistently produces large brook trout and currently holds the Idaho record. Fall fishing for "Mr. Squaretail", dressed in his bright spawning colors, can be quite exciting. For that matter, fishing Henry's Lake any season is always a rewarding experience.

The lake is in the northern part of eastern Idaho, about 18 miles from Yellowstone National Park on Highway 20. From Ennis, Montana take Highway 87 south about 60 miles.

Type of Fish

Cutthroat, Henry's original inhabitant, predominates with brook trout and some hybrid cutbows.

Known Hatches

The main hatch is the Green Damsel in July.

Equipment To Use

Rod: 7 weight, 8 1/2' to 9'.
Line: Fast sinking or slow sinking for shallow areas.
Leaders: 3x to 5x, 9'.
Reel: Mechanical or palm drag.
Wading: It is best to take a boat or float tube. When tubing use chest-high neoprenee waders and fins. *Note:* Thunderstorms can develop suddenly in the area and the shallow lake can become quite dangerous. I once got caught in these conditions and barely got off the lake.

Flies to Use

Wet or nymph patterns: Brown Marabou or Ostrich Leech #4-6, Troth Olive Shrimp #8-12, Olive Damsel Nymph #8-10, Matuka Light and Dark Spruce, Wooly Bugger #8-10. A favorite pattern is one created by Seldon Jones. It's nameless, but sports a peacock body and fuzzy badger hair thorax capped with white raffia. Flies should be weighted and tied a bit bigger and longer.

When to Fish

July through October is very good. Try the "Glory Hole" off Staley Springs, the area between Duck Creek and Hope Creek and the water around A-Frame Bay and Howard Creek. Targhee Creek can be good in the fall.

Season & Limits

The general season is usually the Saturday before Memorial Day weekend to October 31, two fish limit, 5:00 AM-9:00 PM. For exact dates and times check the Idaho department of Fish and Game regulations booklet.

Accommodations & Services

There is lots of camping available at Howard Creek State Park, Staley Springs and at Wild Rose Ranch. A boat ramp and dock is available in A-Frame Bay, Stanley Park, Howard Creek and Stanley Springs. Cabins can be rented at Henry's Lake Lodge. For other services head to the Island Park/Last Chance area.

Rating

Overall, a solid 8.

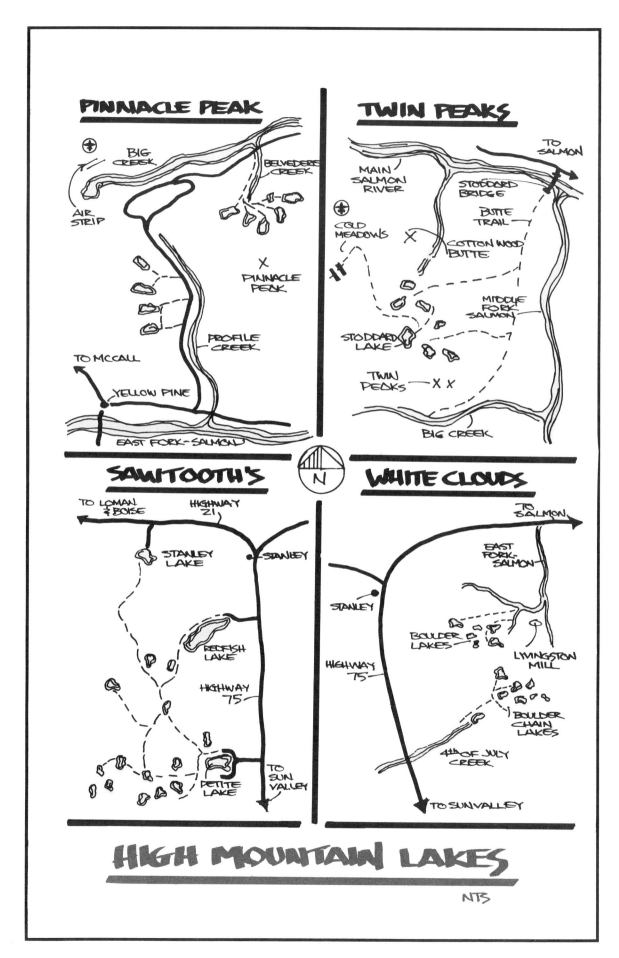

High Mountain Lakes

*I*f you like to hike or backpack and fly fish, Idaho offers some of the best and most picturesque high mountain lake fishing in the country. Generally the farther into the backcountry one goes, the better the chances of finding large fish. With Idaho's beautiful mountain scenery these fly fishing treks are worth the effort, large trout or not.

The majority of the high mountain lakes that are prime fly fishing destinations are located in the state's central wilderness area. Some are quite easy to get to while others require horses or airplanes capable of landing on back country airstrips. See the accompanying maps for some of the best high mountain fly fishing lakes. Note that these maps are not to scale and should be used for fly fishing water locations and not for path finding.

When to Fish

Generally fly fish the high lakes in mid-summer. By October, winter conditions can put an end to fishing.

Type of Fish

Most lakes are stocked with cutthroat, rainbow, brook and golden trout. These populations may be high, but fish size can be small. Restocking occurs every three years.

Equipment to Use

Rods: 5 to 7 weight, 81/2' to 9'.
Line: Floating and sink tip for flexibility.
Leaders: 3x to 6x, 7 1/2' to 9'.
Reel: Palm drag.
Wading: Chest-high, neoprene waders and a float tube is helpful if you want to pack them in.

Flies to Use

At high altitude insect production is decreased, but you'll find caddis (evenings), black midges (especially the pupa stage), freshwater shrimp, leeches, back swimmers, damsels flies, ants and grasshoppers.
Dry Patterns: Parachute and regular Adams #14-20, Henryville Caddis #12-18, Dave's Hopper #10-12.
Nymphs: Black Midge Pupa #16-20, Olive Damsel #10-12, Brown Backswimmer #14-16, Shaggy Otter #12-16, Black, Brown, and Black/Olive Wooly Bugger #8-12.

Hiking

Some areas restrict fires and/or requires portable stoves. Check with the Forest Service. Always carry a topographical map of your hiking area. **DO NOT** use the maps in this book for hiking reference. They're for general use and *are not to scale.* Also, bring out what you take in.

Boulder/White Clouds Area

The White Clouds offer some of the finest back country fly fishing in Idaho. The hike in is relatively easy. Because of nutrient-rich water the areas various lakes are full of insects and hold some very big fish for such high altitude.
The most common way in (and up) is Fourth of July Creek, off Highway 75, south of Stanley, Idaho. The other route is up the East Fork of the Salmon, to Livingston Mill. This route, though a bit steeper, provides access to Boulder and Boulder Chain Lakes. This area does get a lot of visitors, but the jaunt through this mountain range is beautiful and something one will never forget.

Rating

As high lakes go, a 7.5

The Sawtooth Range

These majestic and beautiful granite mountains are often called "America's Alps". Coming from down river, rounding the bend into lower Stanley, the Sawtooth literally explode in your face, presenting a sight that anyone with a sense of the spectacular will always enjoy. This area can get a lot of use in peak season. The most common access to this area are Petit, Redfish, and Stanley Lakes. Petit gets my nod.

Rating:

A 4.

Twin Peaks

This area, deep in the wilderness of Central Idaho, goes by many names: Cottonwood Butte/Stoddard Lake Region, Big Creek or Chamberlain Basin. To simplify things, and because of the two landmark pinnacles, Twin Peaks is a designation that works well.
The lakes in this area, including Stoddard, Kitchen, Cottonwood and Basin, are remote and feature high quality water for fish. As a result, on can find some of the largest backcountry trout in the state. Cutthroat and rainbow 20" or more, unheard of in many other high altitude lakes, can be quite common. In addition, try fishing Big Creek. Good quantities of surprisingly large cutthroat can be found in this creek.
Probably the best way to reach this area is by horse. From Stoddard bridge, which crosses the Salmon River, it's a days ride (or more). On foot it takes a couple of days and covers some 5,500' in elevation. Save your time and take a horse, you'll love it! One can fly into Cold Meadow, though left with a days hike into the lakes. One can also fly into Big Creek and hike in from the south. An area fly shop can help you with these details.

Rating:

The fly fishing is a 10. The trip in, especially if you are hiking makes it a 5.5.

Pinnacle Lakes

I've been very close to these lakes, but because of weather, haven't fished them. Friends who have completed the trek and fly fished this area give it high marks. They found some good trout 16"-17" and lots in the 10"-12" range.

To get to the trail, follow the road out of Yellow Pine, up Profile Creek to Big Creek. The trail head begins where the road crosses Belvedere Creek. On the map, the lakes appear close, but the 3,000' climb can take up to a day and a half. Word has it this can be cut in half by taking Profile Creek over Coin Mountain. In my estimation this route is for the young and fit.

Rating:

From reports, a 6.5.

Pioneer

These lakes are worth considering if you want a handy trip from the Sun Valley area. The Pioneer Mountains and a series of lakes can be reached in a few hours. Some lakes hold trout 8"-10", some don't contain fish at all. But it's a nice trip.

To reach the lakes from Sun Valley/Ketchum take Trail Creek road north and east from town. Turn right on Wildhorse Creek road and look for trail heads or continue along the East Fork of the Big Lost River to Copper Basin road. Trail heads can be accessed off this road.

Rating:

A 3.5.

Comments On
Other Lakes & Reservoirs

Some of the lakes and reservoirs in Idaho fall into this "honorable mention" section because of drought, declining water quality, lack of large trout, access problems and other issues. None the less, these waters have been or are good and one should give them a try.

Cascade Reservoir

Cascade is near McCall, Idaho or 80 miles north of Boise and is probably Idaho's most fished impoundment. Some very large trout are taken here, especially in the spring when the ice goes out. Most of the fish caught in the summer are hatchery raised. Water quality problems may effect the fishery, though time will tell. The reservoir should not be counted out however, as the beauty of the area alone provides great enjoyment for most fly fishers.

Island Park Reservoir

I have always loved fishing the fertile waters of Island Park Reservoir. Many a memorable August afternoon has been spent at the west end, fishing in and off the "finger" areas. Trout of up to 20" were plentiful and fairly easy to catch. But Island Park reservoir has suffered problems, including draw-downs. I'm not sure what size of fish are swimming around the reservoir these days.

Access to the reservoir is quite easy. Most come in from McCrea's bridge on Shotgun Valley road. A boat and motor is needed to access the reservoir downstream from this point. I maintain that the best fishing is at the west end, which is reached from Green Canyon road (Harriman State Park Headquarters) just south of Osborne bridge. If it is "on" Island Park Reservoir is worth a try. At the very least inquire at the fly shops in Last Chance. *Wet and nymph patterns to use:* Brown, Maribou or Ostrich Leech #4-6, Troth Olive Shrimp #8-12, Olive Damsel nymph #8-10, Matuka light and dark Spruce, Wooly Bugger #8-10. Flies should be weighted and tied a bit bigger and longer. Add Caddis pupa imitations when fishing the finger areas.

Lake Lowell

Located 3 miles southeast of Nampa, Idaho, Lake Lowell receives raves for its bass and bluegill fishing. Water conditions can change form year to year however, making fly fishing inconsistent. By early to mid-summer grass and weed growth can make fly fishing a less rewarding experience. With bass in the

4 to 6 pound range and 2 pound crappie, it's hard to argue against fly fishing here. If you're in the area, especially in the late spring when conditions elsewhere are marginal, consider lake Lowell. *Flies to use:* Brown Ostrich, Marabou nymphs #4-6, small leeches, small lead-head jigs, small Griddle Bug in black, brown, bright olive, chartreuse and yellow, #8-10, Foam Spider, Cricket, small popping bugs in black, green, yellow and white #10-12, (#8-10 for crappie). For bass, Wooly Bugger with flashabou, beaded eyes or regular in a variety of colors. Also try streamer patterns imitating chubs and yellow or black perch imitation tied Matuka style.

Mackey Reservoir

This is a very interesting piece of water. It's fed by the Big Lost River and an assortment of area spring creeks that send high quality water into the impoundment. Trout in the 20" plus range are available. With better water and fishing regulation, Mackey could probably rival Henry's Lake as the top reservoir in the state.

Droughts have caused severe draw-downs which tend to concentrate the fish. With few fishing restrictions the trout populations get tested severely making it hard to predict what kind of fishing to expect.

Access to the reservoir is off Highway 93 which parallels it's length. It can be fished from the bank, especially on the west side, but a boat or float tube is the preferred method. July can be very good in the northern end near the shallow backwaters. In and around the mouths of creeks can be good as well. *Flies to use:* Gray Drake nymph, Brown leeches, Black, Brown and Tan Wooly Bugger.

Magic Reservoir

Located 30 miles south of Sun Valley/Ketchum, Magic has fertile water that can produce some very high quality rainbow and brown trout. You probably won't be catching a fish a minute here but you will get into some real tackle-busters.

Drought conditions in the late 1980's and in 1990 have severely affected the reservoirs water supply and adversely affected the fishery. These days, guessing what trout you'll find and what the fishing will be like is a bit of a dice roll. But because this water can be quite rich I would never cross Magic Reservoir off the list, especially in the fall. *Flies to use:* Black, Brown and Variegated Wooly Bugger, Black and Yellow Perch Wolly Bugger, Leech patterns and Stayner Duck Tail nymph.

Silver Creek • Hatch Chart

HATCH	STAGE/ TIME OF DAY	FEB	MAR	APR	MAY	JUN	JULY	AUG	SEPT	OCT	NOV
Ephemera simulans (Brown Drake)	D, S, pm					■					
Ephemerella infrequens (Pale Morning Dun)	S, am—D, pm					■	■	■	■		
Baetis parvus (hagena) (Little Olive Quill)	D, S, am					■	■	■			
Callibaetis sp. (Speckled Dun & Spinner)	D, S, pm					■	■				
Tricorytodes minutus (Trico)	S, am						■	■			
Ephemerella inermis (Small Pale Morning Dun)	D, pm						■	■			
Baetis (Pseudocloeon) edmundsi (Bright Olive Dun)	D, pm							■			
Baetis tricaudatus (Blue Winged Olive)	D, pm								■	■	
Paraleptophlebia debilis (Slate Mahogany Dun)	D, pm								■	■	
Caddis Rhyacophila (Green Caddis)	am					■	■				
Brachyptera (Tan Caddis)	am & pm						■	■			
Midges	All day	■				■	■	■			

S = Spinner Stage
D = Dun Stage

am = Sunrise to Noon
pm = Noon to 6 p.m.
eve = Evening

Big Wood River • Hatch Chart

HATCH	STAGE/ TIME OF DAY	FEB	MAR	APR	MAY	JUN	JULY	AUG	SEPT	OCT	NOV
Drunella (Ephemerella) doddsi (Green Drake)	D, pm						■				
Epeorus longimanus (Western Quill Gordon)	D, pm						■				
Baetis sp. (Blue Winged Olive)	D, pm							■	■		
Epeorus deceptivus (Cream Dun)	D, pm—S, eve						■	■			
Heptagenia elegantula (Pink Dun)	D, pm—S, eve							■	■		
Rhithrogena hageni (West. March Brown)	D, pm								■		
Timpanoga (Ephemerella) hecuba (Red Quill)	D, pm							■			
Serratella (Ephemerella) tabilis (Chocolate Dun)	D, pm							■			
Stoneflies Calineura (Golden Stone)	pm					■	■				
Isoperla, Isogenus sp. (Small Yellow Stone)	pm						■				
Caddis Hydropsyche (Spotted Caddis)	pm, eve						■				
Oecctis (Horned Caddis)	pm, eve						■				
Colossosoma (Tan Caddis)	pm, eve						■				
Hydroptilidae (Microcaddis)	pm, eve						■				

S = Spinner Stage
D = Dun Stage

am = Sunrise to Noon
pm = Noon to 6 p.m.
eve = Evening

Additional Information Sources

Idaho Department Of Fish and Wildlife (IDFW) Offices

Headquarters
600 S. Walnut (Box 25)
Boise, ID 83703
(208) 334-3700

Southwest Region
3101 S. Powerline Rd.
Nampa, ID 83686
(208) 465-8465
Lewiston, (208) 743-6502

Panhandle Region
2750 Kathleen Ave.
Coeur d' Alene, ID 83814
(208) 769-1414

Upper Snake Region
1515 Lincoln Rd.
Idaho Falls, ID 83401
(208) 525-7290
McCall, (208) 634-8137

Southeast Region
1345 Barton Rd.
Pocatello, ID 83204
(208) 232-4703

Salmon Region
1215 Hwy. 93 N.
Salmon, ID 83401
(208) 756-2271
Jerome, (208) 324-4350

24 Hour Angling Hotline: 1-800-ASK-FISH (275-3474)

Bureau of Land Management (BLM) Offices

Idaho State Office
3948 Development Ave.
Boise, ID
(208) 384-3306

Panhandle Region
1808 N. 3rd. Street
Coeur d' Alene, ID 83814
(208) 524-7500

Southeast Region
940 Lincoln Ave.
Idaho Falls, ID 83401
(208) 524-500

Salmon Region
Box 430
Salmon, ID 83467
(208) 756-5400

U.S. Forest Service Offices

Boise National Forest
1750 Front Street
Boise, ID 83702
(208) 364-4100

Payette National Forest
106 W. Park Street
McCall, ID 83638
(208) 634-0700

Sawtooth National Recreation Area
Highway 75
Ketchum, ID 83340
(208) 726-7672

Caribou National Forest
250 South 4th Street
Pocatello, ID 83201
(208) 236-7500

Salmon National Forest
Highway 93 North
Salmon, ID 83467
(208) 756-2215

Jackson, Wyoming
(307) 739-5500

Challis National Forest
HC-63 Box 1671
Challis, ID 83226
(208) 879-2285

Targhee National Forest
420 N. Bridge Street
St. Anthony, ID 83446
(208) 624-3151

Salt Lake City, Utah
(801) 524-5030

Idaho Travel Council

700 West State Street
Boise, ID 83702
1-800-635-7820

References and Other Reading Material

- *Idaho Department of Fish and Game General Fishing Seasons and Rules (Including Steelhead)*, Idaho Department of Fish & Game
- *Idaho Atlas and Gazeteer*, Delorme Mapping
- *Idaho's Top 30 Fishing Waters*, Rendezvous Country Publications
- *Idaho, Montana, Wyoming Tour Book*, American Automobile Association
- *Snake River Country Flies and Waters*, Bruce Staples

Area Fly Shops

SOUTHERN IDAHO

Lee Aikin's Sport Shop
245 N. Main Street
Pocatello, ID 83201
(208) 233-3837

Jimmy's All Season Angler
509 E. Oak Street
Pocatello, ID 83201
(208) 232-3042

Northwest Sports Center
1509 Yellowstone Ave.
Pocatello, ID 83201
(208) 238-0577

Ruel Stayners Sporting Goods
831 Main Ave. East
Twin Falls, ID 83301
(208) 733-8453

Blue Lake Sporting Goods
1236 Blue Lakes N.
Twin Falls, ID 83301
(208) 733-6446

Simerly's General Store
P.O. Box 207
Wendell, ID 83355
(208) 536-6651

NORTHERN IDAHO

Joe Roop's Castaway Fly Shop
3620 N. Fruitland Lane
Coeur d'Alene, ID 83814
(208) 765-3133

Joe Roop's Castaway Fly Shop
210 Sherman Ave.
Coeur d'Alene, ID 83814
(208) 667-5441

Pend Oreille Sport Shop
3100 Hwy 200 East
Sandpoint, ID 83864
(208) 263-2412

WESTERN IDAHO

Stonefly Anglers
625 Vista Ave.
Boise, ID 83705
(208) 338 1333

Bear Creek Outfitters & Fly Shop
6003 W. State Street
Boise, ID 83705
(208) 853-8704

Black Sheep Sporting Goods
5725 Fairview Ave.
Boise, ID 83706
(208) 322-7227

Twin River Angler
1033 West Bannock
Boise, ID 83702
(208) 389-9957

Howard's Tackle Shoppe
1707 Garrity Blvd.
Nampa, ID 83687
(208) 465-0946

Lick Creek Fly Shop
721 Lick Creek Rd.
McCall, ID 83638
(208) 634-2824

Streamside Adventures, Inc.
6907 Overland Road
Boise, ID 83709
(208) 375-6008

South Fork Expeditions
541 Thain Road
Lewiston, ID 83501
(208) 746-8946

Classic Rods of Idaho
5272 Chinden Blvd.
Boise, ID 83714
(208) 378-8040

Intermountain Arms & Tackle
900 Vista Ave.
Boise, ID 83714
(208) 345-3477

Intermountain Arms & Tackle
105 E. Idaho
Meridian, ID 83642
(208) 888-4911

EASTERN IDAHO

Jimmy's All Season Angler
275 A Street
Idaho Falls, ID 83402
(208) 524-7160

Guns & Gear
2627 W. Broadway
Idaho Falls, ID 83403
(208) 525-6446

Ultimate Angler
P.O. Box 21
Swan Valley, ID 83449
(208) 483-2722

Henry's Fork Anglers
HC 66 Box 491
Island Park, ID 83429
(208) 558-7525

J&J Outfitters
P.O. Box 125
Irwin, ID 83428
(208) 523-2277

South Fork Lodge
P.O. Box 22
Swan Valley, ID 83449
(208) 483-2112

B&B Drugs & Fly Shop
2425 Channing Way
Idaho Falls, ID 83404
(208) 523-2277

Area Fly Shops

CENTRAL IDAHO

Bill Mason Outfitters
Sun Valley Mall
P.O. Box 127
Sun Valley, ID 83353
(208) 622-9305

Silver Creek Outfitters
507 N. Main Street
P.O. Box 418
Ketchum, ID 83340
(208) 726-5282

Sun Valley Outfitters
P.O. Box 3400
Sun Valley, ID 83353
(208) 622-3400

McCoy's Tackle Shop
Box 210
Ace of Diamonds St.
Stanley, ID 83278
(208) 774-3377

Lost River Outfitters
620 N. Main
P.O. Box 3445
Ketchum, ID 83340
(208) 726-1706

MONTANA*

Blue Ribbon Flys
315 Canyon Street
W. Yellowstone, MT 59758
(406) 646-7642

Madison River Outfitters
117 Canyon Street
W. Yellowstone, MT 59758
(406) 646-9644

Bud Lilly's Trout Shop
39 Madison Ave.
W. Yellowstone, MT 59758
(406) 646-7801
1(800) 854-9559

Jacklin's Fly Shop
105 Yellowstone
W. Yellowstone, MT 59758
(406) 646-7336

Madiosn River Fishing Co.
P.O. Box 627 - 109 Main
Ennis, MT 59729
1 (800) 227-7127

The Tackle Shop
P.O. Box 625
Ennis, MT 59729
(406) 682- 4263

WYOMING*

Westbank Angler
P.O. Box 523
Teton Village, WY 83025
(307) 733-6483

High Country Flies
P.O. 3432
Jackson, WY 83001
(307) 733-7210

Jack Dennis Sports
P.O. Box 3369
Jackson, WY 83001
(307) 737-3270

Orvis Jackson Hole
P.O. Box 9029
485 W. Broadway
Jackson, WY 83001
(307) 733-5407

*These shops are included because they are in the "Idaho neighborhood", just across the state line, and because they can assist fly fishers headed into Idaho.

About The No Nonsense Authors

Harry Teel

Mr. Teel wrote the first "No Nonsense" fly fishing guide. It highlights fly fishing in Central and Southeastern Oregon and was published in 1993-94.

The guide's format was the result of a collaboration with publisher David Banks. The pair maintained that many books on fly fishing tend to be wordy. Harry also knew (from personal and professional experience) that most fly fishers require only basic information about a particular area or water in order to explore and enjoy it. The continued success of Harry's guide confirm these notions. The principal reason for the guide's popularity however is Harry's vast knowledge of Oregon fly fishing.

For the better part of 60 years Mr. Teel has fly fished in his home state. This started with a journey to the Deschutes River with his father, back in 1933. Over the years his fly fishing appetite has taken him from Alaska to Argentina and most spots in between. But Central Oregon remains one of his most cherished places to cast a fly.

After retirement from a career with CH2M Hill, Mr. Teel opened and operated a fly shop in the Central Oregon town of Sisters. He has since retired (again) which afforded him time to combine his extensive fly fishing experience and years of fishing notes into a guidebook. When not fly fishing, Harry and his wife Dee enjoy grandchildren, travel, golf and visits to or from their many friends.

Bill Mason

When it comes to the Idaho fly fishing business, Mr. Mason has done it all: guide, outfitter, instructor, amateur aquatic entomologist and author. He has fly fished nearly the entire state and now shares this experience with us. This vast knowledge wasn't gained overnight however.

After college, Bill Mason moved from Washington state to Idaho and helped build a major outfitting operation at the Henry's Fork of the Snake River. Here he helped identify most of the key hatches and create appropriate fly patterns, many of which are recognized and used today. Bill also helped start the first fly shop in Boise, Idaho.

Next, at the request of the Sun Valley Company, Bill develop the area's first professional fly fishing school and guiding program. Shortly thereafter, he helped start Snug Fly Fishing, a fly shop he operated for fifteen years. Bill eventually purchased the shop, renaming it Bill Mason Sun Valley Outfitters. Bill has also identified most of the insect hatches and fly patterns relevant to waters in the Sun Valley area.

Bill has written much on the topic of fishing the fly including, *Fly Fishing, Learn from a Master,* published by *Sports Illustrated*. This "how to" book is in addition to numerous articles, a weekly newspaper column and Bill Mason's No Nonsense Guide to Fly Fishing In Idaho.

Bill and his wife Jane are raising their family in the Sun Valley area. This occasionally reduces Bill's time to pursue rising trout. But when the hatch is on Bill either knows about it or is casting to it. Bill also enjoys travel and an occasional round of golf.

About The No Nonsense Guides

No Nonsense guides are a new concept in fly fishing guidebooks. These guides provide basic and essential information, delivered in an easy-to-read format. All the essential questions answered: Where do I go? How do I get there? What do I take? When do I fish? Where can I stay?

No Nonsense authors are experienced local fly fishers who are uniquely qualified to present information about their area waters. The maps in these guides are tidy versions of drawings these authors would sketch if you happened to meet them and ask, "Where can I fly fish around here?".

The fly shops listed in the back pages are excellent places to gather more in-depth fly fishing information. Local "tout" from these shops, combined with the basic insights gleaned from a No Nonsense guide will give you everything you'll need for a successful fly fishing outing short of nice weather and hungry fish.

What is known can always be amended. Your additions to the information in these guides are welcome, as are any other comments you may have concerning No Nonsense guides. Drop a line to:

David Communications • 6171 Tollgate • Sisters, Oregon • 97759

Look for No Nonsense Guides to other popular fly fishing locations.

How To Get 'Em

Harry Teel's No Nonsense
Guide To Fly Fishing
Central & Southeastern Oregon

Twenty popular fly fishing spots in this unique region are highlighted, ranging from the small, spring-fed Fall River to The Metolius and the renowned Deschutes River. There are helpful comments on 20 lesser known fly fishing gems such as Fish Lake, Deep Creek and the Little Blitzen river. The 60 page guide includes detailed maps, drawn by the author and locator and highway maps.

Get your guide at your favorite fly shop, bookstore or order by mail from the publisher. Send your check for $14.95 plus $3.00 shipping and handling to:

David Communications • 6171 Tollgate • Sisters, Oregon • 97759

ISBN#0-9637256-0-2
Please allow two weeks for delivery.

Bill Mason's No Nonsense
Guide To Fly Fishing
In Idaho

The state's 20 most popular fly fishing spots are highlighted ranging from spring-fed creeks in the unique Hagerman area, to the world famous Henry's Fork and Silver Creek. Fly fishing Idaho's High Mountain Lakes are described as are lesser known gems like the Little Wood and Falls Rivers. Key hatch information on the more complex rivers is also provided. The 60 page guide includes detailed maps annotated by the author plus locator and highway maps, hatch charts and more.

Get your guide at your favorite fly shop, bookstore or order by mail from the publisher. Send your check for $14.95 plus $3.00 shipping and handling to:

David Communications • 6171 Tollgate • Sisters, Oregon • 97759

ISBN#0-9637256-1-0
Please allow two weeks for delivery.

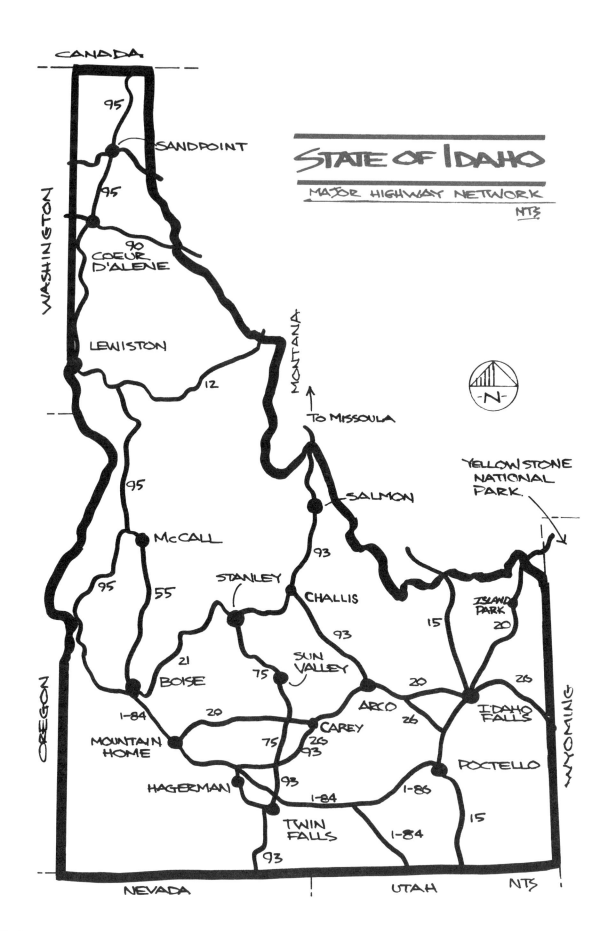

STATE OF IDAHO

MAJOR HIGHWAY NETWORK

NTS